SCHOOLWIDE APPROACHES

FOR

FOSTERING RESILIENCY

Nan Henderson, Bonnie Benard, Nancy Sharp-Light

Editors

Introduction by Barbara Wotherspoon

Published by
Resiliency In Action, Inc.

Copyright © 2000 by Resiliency In Action, Inc.

ISBN: 0-9669394-2-5   3rd Printing

Library of Congress Catalogue Card Number:
00-090817

Clip Art Copyright © 1990-1999, RT Computer Graphics, Inc.
      Rio Rancho, NM. 505-891-1600, www.rtgraphics.com.

Manufactured in the U.S.A.

For more information about this book and other resiliency books and resources, contact:
      Resiliency In Action, Inc.
      P.O.B. 90319
      San Diego, CA 92169-2319
      1-800-440-5171 or Fax: 1-858-581-9231
      www.resiliency.com

CONTENTS

Introduction

Building Resiliency in Atkinson Academy: One School's Journey

by Barbara Wotherspoon

"What can be done in this school to help all children be more successful?" was the question we asked ourselves as a school family about 10 years ago as we evaluated what we did well and was working, and what we needed to do differently. I want to share a little about our school's journey of change to an effective resiliency-building organization–a "community for all learners"–as a way of introducing this book on how schools can effectively foster resiliency in their students.

Our school, Atkinson Academy, is a public elementary school of about 415 students in southern New Hampshire. Its community is a blend of rural and suburban. For most of the 1980s, there was a lot of turnover in leadership at the school (six principals in nine years), which lead to a lack of cohesiveness and shared vision.

Effective change starts when people see the need for change, and when I arrived as another new principal the staff at the Academy was ready to assess the status quo and develop a course of action for improvement. Our needs assessment involved interviews with all staff and about 100 community members. As the new principal, I shared at an organizational meeting the strengths of the staff as told to me by the community. I will always remember the sense of hopefulness that permeated the room when these educators heard their strengths–the feelings community members had shared about what was positive in their school.

When we started our change process, we weren't even thinking of the word "resiliency." We just determined to improve what we did for children in a collegial way, using our scant resources to develop the best teaching and learning environment possible. As we shared and listened to each other–teachers, assistants, other school staff, parents, town leaders, other community members–we developed a common vision that built on what was positive about the school, and we formulated a plan of action to make it better. Learning about resiliency along the way only validated our growing belief in the power of focusing on the positive.

Everyone who touched a child was seen in our common vision as a part of the solution of helping all children become more resilient. Comments such as "all of us are smarter than one of us," "the children belong to all of us," "we are all part of the team," and "we need to talk to Mama Lewis (the cafeteria manager) and John (the head custodian) for their opinions," were indicative of the growing power of our positive, strength-focused approach to change.

Any lasting change in behavior requires a change of attitude and philosophy. The moto our school staff created, "Atkinson Academy: A Community of Learners: We Care, We Share, We Dare!" tells it all. It is this attitude, not any specific program, that made the difference. This attitude is what motivates us to find the key to what will work with any particular child or what we can do to prevent or to overcome any particular problem.

We discovered that the ingredients needed were already in our school. We just needed to put them together and highlight some in such a way as to wrap a web of resiliency builders around each child (see chapter two for an explanation of The Resiliency Wheel and the web of resiliency). It was exciting to discover all we could do for all the children at Atkinson–not just a few at "most risk"–that was positive, hopeful, and powerful. They didn't cost a lot of money, but they have had positive, long-term results.

In addition to utilizing some of the myriad of strategies detailed in this book, examples of the some of the initiatives we developed included:

- Monday Morning Meeting, which brings the whole school family together for 30 minutes the first thing Monday morning in a celebration of our school and the attitudes, strengths, and accomplishments of our children. These student-run ceremonies anchor our school and renew our sense of purpose every week.
- In-service training of teachers and all school personnel in such resiliency-fostering skills as healthy conflict resolution and creating more effective learning and teaching environments, which provide on-going skill development for our staff.
- Student Response Team, a team of caring adults who are available to assist any child who may need to leave a classroom in order to receive support and/or problem solve in order to re-enter the learning environment. In addition, all educators in our school are focused on translating behaviors into an understanding of student needs, and on utilizing what is necessary to meet each student's needs.
- Guardian Angels, a program designed so that each child who may benefit from a mentoring relationship is paired with an adult mentor in addition to the caring connection the child has with his or her classroom teacher.

Whenever our school community is faced with adversity of some kind–a death in a student's family or of a staff member, a challenging parent situation, misunderstandings among school-team members, an error in judgment–we remind each other to look at this as another opportunity to learn to put the child's needs first and to discover how we can work together in a more productive manner.

As we have studied the resiliency-building information, we have seen that it also applies to adults. Applying the resiliency framework to students and adults has taken learning on my part, as I have a tendency to push too hard and be too impatient. I am learning to walk my talk: to respect each person in the school as an individual, to discover each person's strengths and how to best foster his or her resiliency. I now try to view "resistance" as a communication of a need that I haven't yet figured out. "Another opportunity to learn" has also become my personal mantra.

If a school community creates a caring and responsive school climate for children and adults and is respectful of each other, then that modeling and that message becomes infused in all that happens in the school. It can be done classroom by classroom, but–as the improved academic outcomes, reduced discipline problems, and increase in morale at Atkinson has shown–it is stupendous when the whole school buys in and creates this type of change. When everyone in a school community believes they are part of the solution and when strengths are recognized and emphasized, hopefulness becomes the frame of reference. This leads to continual improvement. And that is what resiliency is all about. ✳

Barbara Wotherspoon, principal of Atkinson Academy, just completed a sabbatical leave as Visiting Practitioner at the Harvard University Principal's Center. In addition to her work as a school administrator, she teachers graduate courses related to contemporary critical issues in education and society and she also teaches in the Massachusetts Elementary School Principals Association program for aspiring principals. Barbara provides training across the U.S. in creating resiliency-building school organizations, diversity, inclusive education, multicultural education, and creating safe schools. She can be reached at (603) 382-7503, or by e-mail: leew@tiac.net.

PART ONE

Understanding Resiliency

Resiliency In Schools: Making It Happen

by Nan Henderson, M.S.W.

> *This chapter is adapted from* Resiliency in Schools: Making It Happen for Students and Educators, *by Nan Henderson and Mike M. Milstein published by Corwin Press, 1996. It was originally published in the November, 1997 issue of* Principal *magazine.*

Schools today face difficult challenges in assuring success for all students and fostering an empowered, enthusiastic staff of lifelong learners. A new and hopeful perspective based on resiliency provides a coherent, research-based framework for achieving both of these goals. Longitudinal studies in psychology, psychiatry, and sociology show how children and adults are able to bounce back from stress, trauma, and risk in their lives, and suggest resiliency strategies that are applicable to students and educators.

In recent decades, the focus on at-risk students and the identification if specific risk factors have discouraged those who advocate success for all students. Some believe that multiple risks in children's lives doom an increasing number of children to negative outcomes—dropping out of school, using drugs, going to prison.

> *"Many children identified as 'high risk'* do not *develop the litany of problems educators have come to expect."*

However, resiliency studies—some of which have followed children into adulthood—reveal, even among children exposed to several potent risk factors, "a consistent—and amazing—finding: While a certain percentage of these high-risk children developed various problems a greater percentage...became healthy, competent adults" (Benard, 1991, p. 2).

In short, longitudinal research has corrected an inaccurate impression left by earlier risk research: Many children identified as "high risk" *do not* develop the litany of problems educators have come to expect. Although exposed to high-risk environments, they have proven to be resilient. In addition, a significant number of those who do experience problems in childhood demonstrate resiliency in adulthood.

According to Werner and Smith (1992), authors of the most extensive resiliency study ever conducted in this country, what is needed is "a corrective lens—an awareness of the self-righting tendencies that move children toward normal adult development under all but the most adverse circumstances" (p. 202).

Searching for Resiliency

In the past few years my experience in interacting with thousands of educators about the concept of resiliency, both in themselves and their students, has convinced me that some characteristics of resiliency can be found in everyone—if we look for them with the same meticulousness we use in looking for risks. Many educators tell me that they have recognized the potential of resiliency, and that emerging studies offer validation for their belief that all students have the potential to succeed. These educators have developed a "resiliency attitude," the critical first step in fostering resiliency in schools.

This attitude involves searching for, nurturing, and reinforcing "any scrap" of resilience (Higgins 1994), and examining situations in which students or colleagues "out-maneuvered, outlasted, out-

> *"It seems almost impossible to overcome adversity without the presence of a trusting relationship, even with a single adult."*

witted, or outreached" an adversity (Wolin and Wolin 1993). It also involves the verbal and nonverbal communication of the message, "Your risks, stresses, and problems are not the end of the road. They are only steps on the road of life. Together, we will find ways for you to bounce back."

The Protective Factors

Crucial to the resiliency process is the presence of protective factors—characteristics within the individual or environment that reduce the negative impact of stressful situations and problems (on p.5). Though a few protective factors have genetic roots (such as an outgoing social personality), most of them "can be learned, and thus promoted" (Higgins 1994, p. 22).

While it is impossible to determine how many protective factors any one person needs (some seem to rebound with a few; others need more), it is important to remember that protective factors "make a more profound impact on the life course of children...than do specific risk factors or stressful life events" (Werner & Smith 1992, p. 202). The goal is to build in enough protective factors to offset the impact of stressful life events. When the balance is favorable, successful adaptation—resiliency—is the outcome.

> *"It is important that expectations be both high and realistic to be effective motivators."*

Six Building Blocks of Resiliency

Six consistent themes have emerged from research showing how schools, families, and communities can provide both environmental protective factors and the conditions that foster individual factors (Hawkins & Catalano 1990; Benard 1991).

1. *Increase Bonding.* This involves strengthening connections between the individual and any pro-social person or activity. It is based on evidence that children with strong positive bonds are far less involved in risk behaviors than those without these bonds.

Table 1. Individual and Environmental Characteristics that Facilitate Resiliency

Individual Characteristics	Environmental Characteristics
1. Gives of self in service to others and/or a cause 2. Uses life skills, including good decision-making, assertiveness, impulse control, and problem-solving 3. Sociability/ability to be a friend/ ability to form positive relationships 4. Sense of humor 5. Internal locus of control (i.e., makes decisions based on internal values and beliefs rather than the opinions and pressures of others.) 6. Perceptiveness 7. Autonomy/independence 8. Positive view of personal future 9. Flexibility 10. Capacity for and connection to learning 11. Self-motivation/initiative 12. Is "good at something"; personal competence 13. Feelings of self-worth and self-confidence 14. Personal faith in something greater; spirituality 15. Creativity	1. Promotes close bonds 2. Values and encourages education 3. Uses high warmth/low criticism style of interaction 4. Sets and enforces clear boundaries (rules, norms, and laws) 5. Encourages supportive relationships with many caring others 6. Promotes sharing of responsibilities, service to others, "required helpfulness" 7. Provides access to resources for meeting basic needs of housing, employment, health care, and recreation 8. Expresses high, and realistic, expectations for success 9. Encourages goal-setting and mastery 10. Encourages pro-social development of values (such as altruism) and life skills (such as cooperation) 11. Provides leadership, decision-making, and other opportunities for meaningful participation 12. Appreciates and develops the unique talents of each individual

Adapted from the book, Resiliency in Schools: Making It Happen for Students and Educators by Nan Henderson and Mile Milstein, published by Corwin Press, Thousand Oaks, CA (1996).

One way to increase bonding is to make family involvement a priority by actively recruiting parents, giving them meaningful roles in the school, and calling them periodically with good news about their children. Setting up parent resource centers and giving parents a voice in school governance are other ways of bonding schools and families.

Students need a variety of in-school and before- and after-school activities—art, music, drama, sports, community service, and clubs of all types—for positive connections. Teaching strategies that address multiple intelligences and individual learning styles also increase students' bonds to school and learning.

2. *Set clear and consistent boundaries.* Be consistent in implementing school policies that clarify behavior expectations. These should be clearly written and clearly communicates, and, coupled with appropriate consequences, consistently enforced. This step also works best when incorporated with other resiliency-building steps. For example, it is important to involve students in establishing behavior policy and enforcement procedures (including consequences), but to do so with an attitude of caring rather than punishment.

3. *Teach life skills.* These include cooperation, conflict resolution, resistance and assertiveness skills, communication skills, problem solving, decision making, and healthy stress management. When these skills are adequately taught and reinforced, they help students successfully navigate the perils of adolescence, especially use of cigarettes, alcohol, and other drugs (Botvin & Botvin, 1992). These skills also help to create an environment conducive to learning.

One of the best ways to teach life skills is through cooperative learning, which incorporates skills for getting along. Another way is to have students identify and practice life skills observed in books and plays.

4. *Provide caring and support.* This is the most crucial of all the elements that promote resiliency. In fact, it seems almost impossible to successfully overcome adversity without the presence of a trusting relationship, even with a single adult, that says, "You matter." Family members, teachers, neighbors, and youth workers often can provide this relationship; peers and even pets can also help build resiliency (Werner & Smith 1992; Higgins 1994).

Educational reformers are beginning to recognize the importance of a caring environment as the foundation for academic success. Noddings (1988) notes, "It is obvious that children will work harder and do things—even odd things like adding fractions—for people they love and trust" (p. 32).

Behaviors that express caring and support include noticing all students, knowing their names, drawing out those who may not readily participate, and investigating and intervening when students are dealing with difficult circumstances. Caring and support are also expressed in incentive programs that offer all students chances to succeed, like recognizing them when they bring up a grade or are "caught being good."

5. *Set and communicate high expectations.* It is important that expectations be both high and *realistic* to be effective motivators. Benard (1993) describes several ways schools can implement this step. First, school staff should convey to students messages like, "What I am asking you to do is important; I know you can do it; and I wont give up on you."

Classrooms that embody high expectations are characterized by higher-order, meaningful, and participatory curriculums; flexible, heterogeneous grouping (with little or no tracking or labeling); evaluation systems that reflect multiple intelligences and learning styles; and a variety of participatory activities, including community service opportunities.

Teaching strategies that communicate high expectations are cooperative rather than competitive and focus on interest-based motivation. They place responsibility for learning on students, through active participation and decision making.

6. *Provide opportunities for meaningful participation.* This strategy involves giving students a lot of responsibility for what goes on in school by providing opportunities for them to solve problems, make decisions, plan, set goals, and help others.

The critical foundation for this step is the adoption by educators of an attitude that views students as resources, rather than passive objects or problems. One way to demonstrate this attitude is to put students on governance committees, even in elementary schools. Other approaches to participation include peer-to-peer programs; before-, during-, and after-school activities; and participatory learning strategies.

These six resiliency strategies, when combined, have resulted in increased positive self-concepts, attachment to school, and belief in rules, as well as higher standardized test scores and significant decreases in delinquency, drug use, and suspensions (Hawkins, Catalano, & Miller, 1992). ❈

A MILESTONE STUDY OF RESILIENCY

Child psychologist Emmy Werner and clinical psychologist Ruth Smith began studying all 700 children born on the Hawaiian island of Kauai in 1955. About 200 of these children were considered at high risk due to multiple risk factors such as birthing stress, family dysfunction, poverty, and poor parental education. Of this group, 70 experienced no problems while growing up. The other two-thirds did develop problems, but most were doing well by their mid-30s, according to self-reports, psychological tests, and community records. All but about 30 of the original high-risk group effectively "bounced back."

Based on the findings of their longitudinal study, Werner and Smith have these suggestions for educators fostering resiliency:
- Engage children in acts of required helpfulness.
- Be an optimistic and caring leader/counselor/ facilitator.
- Provide more intensive intervention for those most vulnerable.
- Focus on assessing protective factors, competencies, and strength in addition to weaknesses, deficits, and risks.
- Assure that caring connections continue once a young person leaves your classroom or school.
- Avoid referring to children as being at "high risk"; always use the terminology "from high-risk environments."
- Provide bonding similar to that of an extended family.
- Encourage participation.

References

Benard, B. (1991). *Fostering resilience in kids: Protective factors in the family, school, and community.* Portland, OR: Western Regional Center for Drug-Free Schools and Communities.

Benard, B. (1993). *Turning the corner: From risk to resiliency.* Portland, OR: Western Regional Center for Drug-Free Schools and Communities.

Botvin, G. J., & Botvin, E. M. (1992). Adolescent tobacco, alcohol, and drug abuse: Prevention strategies, empirical findings, and assessment issues. *Journal of Development and Behavioral Pediatrics, 13*,4-24.

Hawkins, J. D., & Catalano, R. F. (1990). *20 Questions: Adolescent substance abuse risk factors* (audiotape). Seattle, WA: Developmental Research and Programs, Inc.

Hawkins, J. D., Catalano, R. F., & Miller, J. Y. (1992). Risk and protective factors for alcohol and other drug problems. *Psychological Bulletin 112:1*, 64-105.

Higgins, G. O., (1994). *Resilient adults: Overcoming a cruel past.* San Francisco, CA: Jossey-Bass.

Noddings, N. (Dec. 7, 1988). Schools face "crisis in caring." *Education Week, 32.*

Werner, E., & Smith, R. (1992). *Overcoming the odds: High risk children from birth to adulthood.* New York, NY: Cornell University Press.

Wolin, S., & Wolin, S. (1993). *The resilient self: How survivors of troubled families rise above adversity.* New York, NY: Villard.

Nan Henderson, M.S.W., is a national speaker and consultant on fostering resiliency and wellness, alcohol and other drug issues, and on organizational change. She has co-authored/edited five books about resiliency, and is the Editor-in-chief at Resiliency In Action, Inc. She can be reached at Nan Henderson and Associates, 5130 La Jolla Blvd., #2K, San Diego, CA 92109, p/f (858-488-5034), or by e-mail: (nanh@connectnet.com).

Fostering Resiliency in Children and Youth: Four Basic Steps for Families, Educators, and Other Caring Adults

by Nan Henderson, M.S.W.

"Where do I *start* in fostering resiliency in my children?" "What are the most important things to do?" "How long does it take?" "What if I only see them once a week (or once a month)?"

Parents and other family members, and educators and other helping professionals, all pose similar questions about resiliency. No one doubts that it is important, even crucial. Almost everyone agrees with my premise that resiliency—"the capacity to spring back, rebound, successfully adapt in the face of adversity, and develop social, academic, and vocational competence despite exposure to severe stress or simply to the stress that is inherent in today's world" (Henderson & Milstein, 1996, p. 7)—is needed by every child alive. Yet often feeling too stretched as it is, family members and helping professionals alike can't imagine fitting one more thing into their already time-pressured interactions with children.

After reading dozens of resiliency-focused studies and books, and after talking with hundreds of kids about their resiliency, I have identified four basic steps to fostering resiliency in children and youth—steps that can be used by all adults, whatever their role in children's lives.

The good news is this: *To a large degree, fostering resiliency occurs by integrating certain attitudes and behaviors with kids into the interactions we already have with them.* This is because fostering resiliency is a *process* that occurs first and foremost in relationships.

When I ask young people who and what contributed to their resiliency (as defined above), they always name individual people first . . . then go on to mention activities, opportunities, classes, or—occasionally—programs. Their relationships with the individuals they name are characterized by the following recommendations:

1. Always communicate "the resiliency attitude." Fostering resiliency begins with an attitude, expressed verbally and nonverbally, that communicates, "I see what is *right* with you, no matter what you have done in the past, no matter what problems you currently face. Your strengths are more powerful than your 'risks.' And whatever risks, problems, and adversity you are facing are steps on the road to bouncing back—they are not the end of the road!"

The Resiliency Attitude is also one in which caring and support is expressed in as many ways as possible—in word and in deed. Listening with compassion, validating the pain of a child's problems while conveying his or her ability to overcome, and providing thoughtful and nurturing gestures—great or small—are all part of this attitude. "She talks to me. She encourages me. She helps me a lot [with my baby]. She lends me money when I need it. She praises me. She tells me she is proud of me," is how 19-year-old Loretta Dejolie described her mother the embodiment of the resiliency attitude (Henderson, 1999a, p. 175).

L.W. Schmick, now attending college, described the attitude of the high school teacher he credits most with his resiliency in this way:

> In my sophomore year, I had an English class with Brian Flynn. A lot of teachers when they see an "at risk" student, they automatically distrust and they don't give them some of the responsibilities they would give other students. But Brian Flynn showed me respect and trust. He gave me a lot of power to take responsibility. He said, "If you want an inch, take an inch. If you want a mile, take a mile." I wasn't set apart as different. He saw me as just another person, not as an "at risk" student (Henderson, 1996b, p. 80).

2. Focus on strengths with the same or an even greater meticulousness as you use in cataloging weaknesses. Steve Wolin (1999) believes that focusing on strengths goes against human nature. I believe it would be easier to do in a strength-reinforcing culture (that is possible to create), which viewed discussing one's capabilities and talents, goals and achievements as positive. A part of this culture would be a good news-reporting media focused equally on all the ways people help, support, sacrifice for, and care for one another. Whether it is because of "nature or nurture"—that old debate!— all adults interacting with young people need training in focusing on strengths, in "cataloguing . . . capabilities with the exquisite concern we normally reserve for weaknesses" (Higgins, 1994, p. 320). I have used a process called The Resiliency Chart outlined in Figure 1 to train myself and others in identifying, reinforcing, nurturing, and using strengths in personal and professional interactions with children and youth.

Figure 1. The Resiliency Chart

For each particular child, draw a t-chart as shown below. On the left-hand side of the chart, list all the concerns—internal, in terms of the attitudes and behaviors of this child, and external, in terms of environmental risks and stressors—that you have about the child. Try to limit your list to a handful of the most pressing problems. On the right-hand side of the chart, list every positive you can think of both within this child and within his or her environment. Think in terms of attitudes, behaviors, personality characteristics, talents and potential talents, capabilities, and positive interests. Think also in terms of the child's environment: List every person, place, organization, or structure that provides positive interaction and support for this child. Referring to Table 1 on page 5 (lists of individual and environmental characteristics that facilitate resiliency) can help with this strength-identification process. Don't limit your thinking, however, to these lists. Include anything you think of as a strength or positive support.

Child's Name_____

Problems/Challenges	Strengths/Positive Supports

The way The Resiliency Chart might look at two different points in one child's life is diagrammed in Table 2 and Table 3. In 1996, I wrote an article about Juanita Corriz, a 15-year-old ninth grader in Santa Fe, New Mexico, who—after a two-year wait—was matched with a Big Sister, Sharyn Obsatz, when she was 14 (Henderson, 1999c). When I talked with Juanita, it became clear that her life had changed significantly for the better in the two years since she met Sharyn—that her strengths evident at age 12 had been nurtured, that others had emerged, and that many of the "risks" in her life had been *mitigated* by this growing list of positive personal and environmental characteristics.

Table 2. Juanita, age 12

Problems/Challenges	Strengths/Positive Supports
1. Single-parent mom who must work every night, and who has several children to care for 2. No father in her life—has never known her dad 3. Lots of unsupervised time on her hands 4. Family history of many people—"including about 20 cousins" —not graduating from high school 5. Family history of poverty 6. Struggling with some of her schoolwork	1. Mom who gives message, "Become something better for yourself" and, recognizing her children's need for more quality adult time, contacted Big Brothers/Big Sisters 2. Example set by mom of getting off of welfare 3. Oldest of four children, recognition that "I am a role model for the others" 4. "Required helpfulness" role (see Werner, 1996) in helping with younger children 5. Desire to do well in school 6. Very giving of self to mom and younger siblings 7. Sociability—outgoing, friendly, enthusiastic 8. Interest and ability in foreign languages 9. Insight about what she needs to do well

It is important to note that families often *simultaneously* contribute risk and strengths in a child's life—a point almost entirely overlooked in the dysfunctional family model. In Juanita's case, her mother is a high school drop out, who got pregnant as a teenager, and who survived for many years on welfare—and now works nights as a custodian to support her family. But this same mother communicates to her children by example and by word, "Make a better life for yourself." Recognizing her own time limitations, she made the call to Big Brothers/Big Sisters that provided both Juanita and one of her younger brothers with mentors.

Two years later, as a result of weekly interactions with her Big Sister Sharyn, whom Juanita describes as "a best friend . . . I've grown to love, who gave me the belief, 'I'm going to try to do good because I know I can do good'" (Henderson, 1999c, pp. 107-108), I would modify Juanita's chart as shown in Table 3.

It is not possible, nor even desirable in preparing a child to successfully cope with life, to eliminate 100% of the risks, stresses, challenges in his or her life. What can be done, through interactions with family members and other caring adults, is to increase "the right hand side of the chart" by focusing on and adding to

Table 3. Juanita, age 15

Problems/Challenges	Strengths/Positive Supports
Delete # 3 from Table 2 Delete # 6 from Table 2	Add the following: 10. Weekly interaction for several hours with a Big Sister who conveys The Resiliency Attitude 11. A certain belief by Juanita that she will go to college 12. Over a 1.5 raise in G.P.A. 13. Increased time reading, due to Big Sister's influence 14. Expansion of altruism to include goal of one day being a Big Sister herself

strengths and environmental supports, which *mitigate* the impact of risk factors and stress. The balance is thereby shifted: The power of the risks and problems are reduced and the strengths—including talents, competencies, resiliency characteristics, and environmental supports—grow.

3. Build a Resiliency Wheel around each child. After communicating a resiliency attitude, after assessing and figuring out how to reinforce, nurture, and expand on strengths, the next step—which can happen simultaneously with the first two—is to build a web of resiliency-fostering environmental conditions around each child. This web is diagrammed in The Resiliency Wheel shown in Figure 2. This Wheel is in actuality a web of protection, support, and nurture of each child's "self-righting tendency" (Werner & Smith, 1992) and capacity for resiliency. No child can have too many strands in his or her web and most today have far too few.

Risk factor research, which encompasses hundreds of studies over several decades, (Hawkins, Catalano, & Miller, 1992) suggests three main strategies—elements one, two, and three of The Resiliency Wheel—for mitigating the impact of risk in the lives of children and youth, in effect moving them towards resiliency (Hawkins & Catalano, 1990). Summarized from chapter one, these are:

Increase Bonding. This involves increasing the connections between young people and resiliency-fostering peers and adults and between young people and any prosocial activity (such as sports, art, music, drama, community and/or school service, and reading and other learning).

Set clear and consistent boundaries. This involves the development and consistent implementation of family rules and norms, school policies and procedures, and community laws and norms. These expectations should be developed with input from young people, clearly communicated (in writing is ideal), and coupled with appropriate consequences that are consistently enforced. My experience as a clinical social worker working with families has shown me that often parents believe that their children know the family rules and what consequences to expect if they are broken, when in the children's minds there is no clarity or consistency about them. Recent experiences with groups of young people in schools has

Figure 2.
The Resiliency Wheel

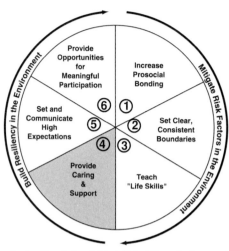

Reprinted from *Resiliency in Schools: Making It Happen For Students and Educators*
by Nan Henderson and Mike Milstein, published by Corwin Press, Thousand Oaks, CA, 1996.

emphasized that here, too, kids *often* experience inconsistency and a laxness—which they complain to me about in our meetings!

Teach "life skills." These include cooperation, healthy conflict resolution, resistance and assertiveness skills, communication skills, problem solving and decision making, and healthy stress management. When these skills are adequately taught and reinforced, they help young people successfully navigate the perils of adolescence, including resisting the use of cigarettes, alcohol, and other drugs (Botvin & Botvin, 1992), and successfully dealing with hurtful peer or adult behaviors.

The life-span focused resiliency research yields three additional steps (synthesized by Benard, 1991)—elements four, five, and six of The Resiliency Wheel—that are consistently shown to help young people "bounce back" from risk, stress, and adversity. Summarized from chapter one, these are:

Provide caring and support. This includes providing unconditional positive regard and encouragement. Because it is the most critical of all the elements that promote resiliency, it is shaded on The Resiliency Wheel. In fact, it seems almost impossible to successfully "overcome" adversity without the presence of caring. This caring does not necessarily have to come from biological family members—though that is ideal. Optimally, every child should have several adults he or she can turn to for help (Benson, Galbraith, & Espeland, 1994). Educational reformers are recognizing the criticalness of a caring environment as the foundation for academic success. Noddings (1988) notes, "It is obvious that children will work harder and do things—even odd things like adding fractions—for people they love and trust" (p. 32).

Set and communicate high expectations. This step appears consistently in both the resiliency literature and in the research on academic success. It is important that expectations be both high and *realistic* to be effective motivators. In reality, however, many children, especially those stuck with one or more of the myriad of labels used in schools and agencies, experience unrealistically low expectations and adopt low expectations for themselves.

Provide opportunities for meaningful participation. This strategy means providing opportunities for problem solving, decision making, planning, goal setting, and helping others, and involves adults sharing power in real ways with children. This resiliency builder is also increasingly showing up in school change literature with expectations that teaching become more "hands-on," curriculum more "relevant" and "real world," and decision making site-based, actively involving all members of the school community (Cooper & Henderson, 1995).

One way that a family member or other concerned adult can use The Resiliency Wheel is by filling in the grid shown in Figure 3, The Resiliency Web, for each child. Again, the goal is to weave as many "strands" in each area, recognizing that due to an individual's circumstances, most of the strands in one or several of the six elements of the Wheel may come from the family, or the school, or the community—rather than being equally distributed across each of these environments.

Once this grid is complete, where should a parent or other adult start in making use of this information? Start where you see the greatest need and/or start wherever you can. Often, as in the case of teacher Brian Flynn, who guided L.W. Schmick and his peers through a community service project, one action will embody many of the elements of The Resiliency Wheel. It is important to recognize that there is no way to know just how much of this web is needed by any one individual to assure "shifting the balance" to a resilient outcome. Most resilient kids who have been studied didn't have a strong web in their family, school, *and* community environments. Some have only a few strands in just a few places. So, start wherever you can based on your assessment of what would help an individual child the most and based on available resources.

Children do need both quantity and quality of resiliency-fostering interactions. Yet, feeling they don't have enough time to give, parents and other adults often underestimate the power of what they can do. As Higgins (1994) notes:

> Several subjects in [my] study [of the resilient] strongly recommended that those of you who touch the life of a child constructively, even briefly, should *never* underestimate your possible corrective impact on that child . . . . In fact, one of the strongest leitmotifs rippling through the interviews [I conducted with resilient survivors] was the reparative power of simple, open availability . . . . Remember, too, that the surrogates [caring adults outside the immediate family] of the resilient were generally available for only small amounts of clock time, and some faded after a limited developmental exposure. Yet their positive impact persisted for life (pp. 324-325).

4. Never Give Up! Resiliency is a life-span process and it ebbs and flows throughout an individual's life. Many resilient survivors of difficult childhood circumstances share how crucial persistence by caring people around them was in their ability to both become resilient and maintain their resiliency. Leslie Krug went through ninth grade in a traditional high school three times before succeeding on the fourth try in her alternative school. She, too, credits her mother as a major source of resiliency. "She just kept making me go to school. She wouldn't let me drop out,"

Leslie said in an interview. She reported that during years of skipping school and "hanging out" her mom got mad at her for her behavior but she never gave up on her. No matter what, her mom was "just always there" (Henderson, 1999d, p. 22).

Figure 3. The Resiliency Web

Child's Name_____

By whom/ what? How?	Prosocial Bonding	Clear, Consistent Boundaries	Life Skills Taught/ Practiced	Caring and Support Provided	High Expectations Communicated	Opportunities for Meaningful Participation/ Contribution
In the Family						
In School						
In the Neighborhood						
In the Community						

Phil Canamar's story (Henderson, 1996e) shows how each of the four steps discussed in this article helped him change from a gang and drug-involved 16-year-old school dropout to a high school graduate involved in soliciting grants from companies such as Honeywell to help "multicultural youth." Phil, too, had a single-parent mother who worked overtime to support her three children. He began getting into trouble in middle school when he experienced a void of caring, supportive adult interaction. This void, he said, contributed to his gang involvement, which he initiated at a time when he said to himself, "No one is here for me. I'm sick of it." He said "I turned toward the gang to find support" (p. 23). Eventually, he dropped out of school and he ran away from home.

His life began turning around when he reconnected with Joe, a former male friend of his mother's who had told him if he ever needed help to contact him. He eventually moved in with Joe and Joe's parents, all three of whom he considers his family. He reports that they give him love and care, support, and encouragement. Phil also contacted an alternative school he had heard about years before. On the day of his initial contact, the principal encouraged Phil to attend, telling him "I know you are a good kid."

"The structure of the school"—which is built around adult and student cooperative teams, experiential activities, identifying and nurturing strengths, finding real-world work placements as part of learning— "the environment here, and last—but not least—my teacher Kathryn who always [for several years] gave me encouragement to take it one day at a time," (p. 23) are the reasons Phil says he succeeded in school. His goal is to one day own his own video production company.

"Facilitating resiliency is more a matter of orientation than specific intervention," writes Higgins (1994, p. 319), based on her study of resilient survivors of childhood trauma. It is clear that fostering resiliency doesn't just happen as a result of putting kids through a program, though many programs such as Big Brothers/Big Sisters, as well as families, provide this crucial "resiliency orientation." A "resiliency orientation" is something all caring adults, however and wherever they interact with children, can convey—through an attitude of optimism and encouragement, a focus on strengths, a commitment to weaving strands from The Resiliency Wheel into children's lives, and persistence, for decades if necessary, in these approaches. ✴

References

Benard, B. (1991). *Fostering resiliency in kids: Protective factors in the family, school, and community.* Portland, OR: Western Regional Center for Drug-Free Schools and Communities.

Benson, P., Galbraith, J., & Espeland, P. (1994). *What kids need to succeed: Proven, practical ways to raise good kids.* Minneapolis, MN: Free Spirit Publishing.

Botvin, G., & Botvin, E. (1992). Adolescent tobacco, alcohol, and drug abuse: Prevention strategies, empirical findings, and assessment issues. *Journal of Developmental and Behavioral Pediatrics, 13* (4), 29.

Cooper, C., & Henderson, N. (1995). *Motivating schools to change: Integrating the threads of school restructuring.* Tasmania, Australia: Global Learning Communities.

Hawkins, J., & Catalano, R. (1990). *20 questions: Adolescent substance abuse risk factors* (Audiotape). Seattle, WA: Developmental Research and Programs, Inc.

Hawkins, J., Catalano, R., & Miller, J. (1992). Risk and protective factors for alcohol and other drug problems. *Psychological Bulletin, 112* (1), 64-105.

Henderson, N., & Milstein, M. (1996). *Resiliency in schools: Making it happen for students and educators.* Thousand Oaks, CA: Corwin Press.

Henderson, N. (1996a). Loretta Dejolie: A teen mom builds a better life for her daughter. In N. Henderson, B. Benard, & N. Sharp-Light (Eds.), *Resiliency in action: Practical ideas for overcoming risks and building strengths* (pp. 175-176). Rio Rancho, NM:Resiliency In Action, Inc.

Henderson, N. (1996b). L.W. Schmick: Challenging the "at risk" label. In N. Henderson, B. Benard, & N. Sharp-Light (Eds.), *Resiliency in action: Practical ideas for overcoming risks and building strengths* (pp. 79-80). Rio Rancho, NM:Resiliency In Action, Inc.

Henderson, N. (1996c). Juanita Corriz: A relationship with a big sister taught her to "want everything there is good for me in life." In N. Henderson, B. Benard, & N. Sharp-Light (Eds.), *Resiliency in action: Practical ideas for overcoming risks and building strengths* (pp. 107-108). Rio Rancho, NM:Resiliency In Action, Inc.

Henderson, N. (1996d). Leslie Krug: "I've been in so much trouble and I'm still here." In N. Henderson, B. Benard, & N. Sharp-Light (Eds.), *Resiliency in action: Practical ideas for overcoming risks and building strengths* (pp. 21-22). Rio Rancho, NM:Resiliency In Action, Inc.

Henderson, N. (1996e). Phil Canamar: "I feel the pain and anger in everybody's heart that joins a gang." In N. Henderson, B. Benard, & N. Sharp-Light (Eds.), *Resiliency in action: Practical ideas for overcoming risks and building strengths* (pp. 22-24). Rio Rancho, NM:Resiliency In Action, Inc.

Higgins, G. (1994). *Resilient adults: Overcoming a cruel past.* San Francisco, CA: Jossey-Bass.

Noddings, N. (1988). Schools face "crisis in caring." *Education Week,* December 7, p. 32.

Richardson, G., Neiger, B., Jensen, S., & Kumpfer, K. (1990). The resiliency model. *Health Education, 21* (6), 33-39.

Werner, E., & Smith, R. (1992). *Overcoming the odds: High risk children from birth to adulthood.* New York, NY: Cornell University Press.

Werner, E. (1996). How children become resilient: Observations and cautions. *Resiliency In Action 1* (1), 18-28.

Wolin, S., & Wolin, S. (1993). *The resilient self: How survivors of troubled families rise above adversity.* New York, NY: Villard Books.

Nan Henderson, M.S.W., is a national speaker and consultant on fostering resiliency and wellness, alcohol and other drug issues, and on organizational change. She has co-authored/edited five books about resiliency, and is the Editor-in-chief at Resiliency In Action, Inc. She can be reached at Nan Henderson and Associates, 5130 La Jolla Blvd., #2K, San Diego, CA 92109, p/f (858-488-5034), or by e-mail: (nanh@connectnet.com).

Reflections From a Pioneer in Prevention, Positive Youth Development, and Education Reform: An Interview with Jeanne Gibbs

by Bonnie Benard, M.S.W.

Creating educational systems that promote and support human development has been the focus of the *Tribes* process for social development and cooperative learning for over 20 years. *Tribes* was conceived by Jeanne Gibbs in the early 1970s, when the predominant responses to problems like substance abuse were "scary films, talks by former addicts, and information on the perils of drug use." This visionary intuited that, "Building positive environments within schools and families not only would be preventive, but could be significant in promoting academic learning and social development" (1995, p. 399). Since then the *Tribes* small group process has spread nationally and internationally and has been used not only in schools but in alcohol recovery centers, juvenile facilities, convalescent homes, daycare centers, and in peer helping and recreational programs. Gibbs' latest edition of the *Tribes* manual incorporates resiliency research, stating that, "The primary mission of *Tribes*...is to assure the healthy development of every child in the school community so that each has the knowledge, skills, and resilience to be successful in our rapidly changing world." According to Gibbs, "This can happen when schools engage all teachers, administrators, students, and families in working together as a learning community—a community dedicated to caring and support, active participation, and positive expectations for all of the young people in their circle of concern" (1995, p. 402).

BB: You have been a real visionary in the prevention and education fields. How did you come to your human development perspective—which often now is called youth development or resiliency?

JG: We were actually just talking "drug education" in the mid-70s. When I became the drug education coordinator for a county health services department in California, I was appalled that what our 18 school districts expected us to do was to run around with pharmacology kits to tell kids about drugs! Now several things—besides my intuition—led me to believe this wasn't the way to go. First of all, my own common sense as a mother: When I walked into my kids' classrooms there was often an essence of caring and interest that told me they would be okay. This got me interested in the whole issue of school climate, which started my search for research.

Also, as my children were growing up, I was a very active volunteer both in the school and in youth organizations like the scouts. It was there that I discovered how the leader's management style affected the participation of the group. In schools, I saw a lot of weary teachers! Also my husband was a businessman who was talking to me about the management research on group and team development. This led me not only into the research on group and organizational development, but also into personally participating in a management training group for a year. At the close of the year, I realized that I was changing. In fact, all the members of the group began to talk about the changes we saw in ourselves: Some of the brash leader types had become considerate, and were listening and caring. Those who were on the quiet side, like myself, had actually become leaders. I was fascinated, and hooked on human and group development. Then I had the opportunity to take an educational training consultant course at the National Training Laboratory in Maine for three weeks one summer. It was an intensive course on how you apply participatory and team management to education. I wondered why we were not using such a process in education.

> *The primary mission of* **Tribes** *is to assure the healthy development of every child in the school community so that each has the knowledge, skills, and resilience to be successful in our rapidly changing world."*

One last major influence moving me to develop the *Tribes* process was my discovery of Urie Bronfenbrenner's books. His *Two Worlds of Childhood* contrasted the extensive use of group learning in Russian schools with the highly individualized, competitive nature of education in the U.S. It also made clear to me the importance of children learning interpersonal skills.

When Bronfenbrenner published *Ecology and Human Development*, which discussed how positive human development moves from micro to macro systems and outward to the world, I was a fan for life. It shifted my whole focus from trying to shape up kids to improving the ecology around them, the environmental systems that impact their lives. I saw that the definition of human development is the move from "Me" to "We" to "Society."

BB: Since you are clearly an open, evolving person—who also reads the research—I'm assuming that the *Tribes* process has also evolved over its 20 year history.

JG: Our early work on *Tribes* began in 1974 with one little grant from the California Department of Education to try the process in one school. At that time I was not into changing the system of the classroom as much as trying to build inter- and intrapersonal skills like self-esteem, decision-making skills, and goal-setting for positive futures. *Tribes* focused on individual change rather than environmental—where it is now.

We now have an assessment process—an action research approach that enables schools to see if they're implementing all components of *Tribes*. We have teachers identify three outcomes, academic and behavioral, that they hope to achieve over time.

I'm convinced the only way we can change systems—a family, a staff that isn't working well together, a school, a classroom, a support group—is to teach people to "stop the action" and to look at the system. Once they can name what is going on, then they can move to the next step. I don't think systems will change until more of our micro and macro systems have that capacity. Think of our political situation. We don't dare to stop action enough, and say to the American public, "Is this good for us? What's going on? What can we change?" This is a critical skill that has to be taught and practiced. It has always been an essential element of *Tribes*.

BB: It seems to me that the human development approach—the very idea that prevention and education should be focused on creating environments that meet youth's developmental needs for belonging, respect, power, and meaning—has always been somewhat counter cultural in the U.S. Do you see any signs that it is moving more to the mainstream of prevention and education?

JG: I think that we're coming close to it now. If we can weave all of the knowledge, all of the great research we now have—and didn't have in the 1970s—about human development, brain compatible learning, cooperative learning, multiple intelligences, and resiliency, into creating ideal learning environments, then we will finally be able to improve American education.

We know from brain compatible learning research that kids cannot learn when in fear, when not feeling safe, when feeling mistrustful. The brain down shifts. We have too many classrooms that do not have an environment of safety, trust, and kindness. Yet we know from resiliency research that no matter where a youngster comes from, whatever the family or neighborhood situation, if a youth can walk into a school and feel safe and cared for, he or she will learn. Our brains shift from that reptilian place upward to where the mind can think clearly.

In *Tribes*, we train teachers to help students make this shift. A community circle begins every day, so that everyone gets to share, "Something special has happened for me," or "Something was exciting," or "What I hope and dream is....." It's very important to know that's how learning happens, that if we have controlling environments—expecting kids to memorize, regurgitate, and compete in an individualistic type of way—they will not achieve. It is that supportive environment that conditions taking in information and being able to think it through constructively and critically. It's very exciting to hear kids learn to give appreciation to others in their group—when they can tell others what special gifts they gave the group in order for them to work together. By appreciating the uniqueness of each individual within a group, we're building the strengths—rather than focusing on weaknesses or criticism—that help kids soar.

BB: Tell us a little about some of the international applications of *Tribes*.

JG: One of the most unique is in Slovakia, in Bratislava, at the demonstration school at the Slovak Academy of Sciences. They discovered *Tribes* when they sent two professors over about five years ago. They believed that they could not establish democracy in a state system that's been totalitarian for 40 years unless they, as instructors, knew what democracy is. These two beautiful women professors sat there and said, "We ourselves were not permitted to make decisions. How can we, then, help a new population do that?" We assisted in translating *Tribes* in 1987, and then they got a small grant from the Sauros Foundation so one of our trainers could train a cadre of their teachers.

In Scotland, for about the last four years, there's been an effort to move from regimented education to more of an emphasis on human development and caring systems. An educator from Scotland went through one of our training sessions, went back and has *Tribes* going well in the Northern Isles of Scotland.

The *Tribes* process is also being used by the Ojibwa Nation of Ontario and Manitoba, Canada. Before Laura Horton, a beautiful Ojibwa educator, took *Tribes* to her people she consulted with one of the Elders, Anne Wilson, "What do you think? Would this be appropriate for our people?" Anne responded, "We have lost this in our children. It's the Old Ways—the old ways of caring, of being there, of being concerned and taking care of each other." It is about community.

BB: Well, Jeanne, you are certainly a respected Elder in this field. Since you told me last year that you have finally given up the idea of retirement and are going "to work to create systems change in schools," you must have hope that change is possible and worth continuing to work for.

JG: It is happening, Bonnie, it is absolutely happening. Every school in Honolulu is moving this way. The Superintendent of the Department of Education of Hawaii has created a "Success Compact" which shifts the focus to instruction in relationships and community. We think at some point, every school in Hawaii will be a *Tribes* school.

Yes, people are finally saying we have to turn to a whole different sort of approach and philosophy of youth development. I am very hopeful and even confident that education will change.

BB: It is certainly a testament to your vision and the compelling work you've done for 20 years—work for which all of us who believe in human development and resiliency feel extremely grateful to you. Thank you for shining your light on the path! ✳

Jeanne Gibbs' 1995 edition of Tribes: A New Way of Learning and Being Together *(432 pages) is available through CenterSource Systems, 305 Tesconi Circle, Santa Rosa, CA 95401. Phone: 707-577-8233. Fax: 707-526-6587. E-mail:(centrsrc@aol.com). For information on training, phone 415-289-1700.*

Don't Tell the Neighbors: A Principal Tells His Personal Story

by Ted N. Okey, Ph.D.

My goal is to share how the language and theories of resiliency relate to many educators' lives. I began attending resiliency workshops three years ago. My reason for getting involved was that I was searching for ways to help turn around an impoverished school, one making the papers for student walkouts and for gang behavior. I was arriving as the fourth principal in five years. I knew I was going to need some new skills and ideas to work with the parents, community, and staff to make this an effective school. Little did I know that the training would give me a new language for understanding the unfolding of my own life and that of my family.

Principal, Ted Okey, visiting in his office with student members of the school's K-Nite news.

I have spoken in several states and overseas about dropout prevention and at-risk youth, but I have never told my own story. I rarely reference my younger sister's dropping out as the motivation for doing a doctoral study on the family perspective of dropping out. Our family of six: mom, dad, older brother, two younger sisters, and I, averaged less than a year in each new home. One of the patterns in my growing up was frequent moves, rarely knowing neighbors or making friends beyond a superficial level. I attended 11 elementary schools. I was scripted to live a life following the rules of the dysfunctional family, "Don't talk, don't trust, don't feel." I learned to use an extrovert nature and sense of humor to keep people distant and to handle relationships without ever sharing my inner self.

> "I have spoken in several states and overseas about dropout prevention and at-risk youth, but I have never told my own story."

Introversion and withdrawal were the coping mechanisms for my mother. I grew up under a father's orders to keep the truth about life in our home secret. No one was to know that my mother was a psychotic manic depressive. His narcissism and his need to be viewed as highly successful made it urgent that mom's illness be kept a secret. What it took years of therapy and training for me to understand, and tragically, what he never understood, was that the true dark family secret was his verbal abuse of my mother, his violence and anger toward his four children, and his narcissistic personality disorder.

My wife and I grew up as next door neighbors. When we reunited after not seeing each other for 17 years, she remarked that she always pictured the Okeys as the perfect family. She remembers me as a cute blonde-haired boy, with a surfer brother and two pretty little sisters. She remembers the house with the pool, dad and his business suits and his big Pontiac, always seeming so friendly and proper. We never spoke about our family problems, so she didn't realize I grew up in a world in which I could never return a friend's favor of having him sleep over, could never have a birthday party, and could never bring a girl friend to meet my parents.

The Language of Resiliency Provides Personal Explanations

I was 40 years old before I understood the unfolding of my mother's life. It wasn't until I learned the language of resiliency that I was able to explain it. Shirley Leone Brickley was born April 9, 1923. She was the first daughter of Ted and Nell Brickley. Nell was the oldest daughter of the once wealthy Dearborn family of Stone City, Iowa. Ted was the only and illegitimate son of Tess Brickley, a mildly retarded Irish girl whose father Red committed suicide after his farm failed in the late 1800s, leaving her to be a servant and housekeeper in town. During that time she was raped, gave birth, and was sent to live with her younger sister Vonnie. Tess never left Vonnie's home, living to be 94, and was the only great grandparent I ever knew.

> *"At age 11, I came home from school to find my mother sobbing at the kitchen table. I cried with her, not knowing why. The tears, according to mom, had no explanation. The crying grew into days and weeks of not getting out of bed."*

Life was good for my mother. Her father worked as the electrician at the reformatory in Anamosa, Iowa. Nell worked as a nursing assistant at the Catholic hospital in town. Shirley was given dance and singing lessons and went from party to party performing for family and friends. She was a bright, beautiful, and remarkable child in every way.

At age seven, her sister Lois was born. Lois was small and unhealthy and took a great deal of Nell's time. The year mom turned 14 Lois contracted polio. The brutal surgery of the time left her with a shortened leg and a scarred body. She was told she would never bear children. Mother was sent to live next door with her Aunt Vonnie. In her 18th year, her father died suddenly from an aneurysm. She left home and joined the Navy. She met my father, and seven days after meeting while he was on leave in Kansas City, they married.

For the first 11 years of my childhood, my mother was the greatest mom who ever lived. My life was filled with games and reading stories, playing cards, and visiting relatives. When I began playing baseball, my mother would watch games with my brother and me, learning player's names, like Snider and Mays and Williams and Mantle. She would make games of naming the players on a team or alphabetically.

Ted Okey fosters resilience in his students, no matter where they are... in the lunchroom, in the classroom, or outside after school.

In 1957, after a fight with his boss and quitting his personnel job in anger, my father moved us to California. For my mother, visits with her Iowa family ended. Two years later, when I turned 10, Tess and Vonnie died within a year of one another. We made trips back to Iowa for the funerals. Those were our last trips together as a family.

At age 11, I came home from school to find my mother sobbing at the kitchen table. I cried with her, not knowing why. The tears, according to mom, had no explanation. The crying grew into days and weeks of not getting out of bed, followed by manic weeks of furniture polishing and ironing the sheets and handkerchiefs twice a day. When my youngest sister began school, my mother gave up her final connections to reality and retreated into a world of Librium, shock treatments, and long stays in Brentwood Veteran's Hospital. She has lived there, off and on, for the past 35 years. She has no teeth, is fed through her stomach, and often doesn't recognize me when I visit.

As I look back at my mother's life, I find in the language of resiliency a plausible explanation for her retreat into mental illness. The great trauma of my mother's life was her sister's polio. Nell Brickley, a deeply religious Irish Catholic, believed that God had punished the family for indulging my mother. That punishment was to cripple their second child, Lois. Therefore, my mother was sent away to live with Aunt Vonnie, while Lois was raised in a world of nurture and support. Lois went on to get a college education, to teach, and has five grown children. My mother's response was to stop doing anything her sister couldn't do. She gave up dance, refused to swim, would not golf or bowl; in short, she would do nothing requiring the use of her legs.

> *"It is painfully clear that my mother could count very few external or internal assets. Those she could count were no longer being nurtured. Her answer was to retreat into mental illness."*

As long as she had Vonnie and her father, mom had loving caring relationships. I believe their deaths, the move to California, and living her life solely for her children resulted in a stripping away of her external and internal assets/protective factors. When the last of her four children left for school, she gave up. She was cut off from emotional support and had no outside community interests to empower her. She lived as little more than a fifth child under my father's rigid control. She gave up reading and learning, became fearful of even the simplest card party or gathering, and finally, lost her esteem and her sense of purpose or future. My father retreated into working two jobs and was having an affair with his secretary when they divorced.

As I review the lists of personal resiliency builders and environmental resiliency builders (see p. 5), it is painfully clear that my mother could count very few. Those she could count were no longer being nurtured. Her answer was to retreat into mental illness.

I have never shared my story publicly. When I speak at conferences, I am introduced from a biography that lists degrees and titles and accomplishments. On the face of things, one would conclude that I am successful. I present as a successful middle-aged educator. What I do not put on my resume is the story of my family, my mother's mental illness, my father's physical and verbal abuse, and the years of hiding our family secrets. I do not disclose the resulting insecurities, the sessions of therapy, or the years of anger and bitterness at having been deserted by both parents.

> *"Three particular teachers took a special interest in me and advocated for me throughout high school. They were examples of those rare individuals who see what is not told or shared."*

Why I Didn't Succumb

The reality is that my formal list of accomplishments means very little compared to the real happiness of my life, which grows from a loving wife and a beautiful 12-year-old son. When I look back on the last 14 years of my life, my marriage, my child, my love of education, I feel I was given a second chance in life. Resiliency theory explains much of the reason I reached that second chance and did not succumb to self-destructive behavior and addictions.

Unlike my mother, I did not separate myself from my connections to family. I still make return visits to all of my living relatives. When my son was three I took him to visit Stone City and Anamosa and introduced him to all his living relatives there.

Further, I found efficacy, caring, and high expectations in my education. Despite going to 11 elementary schools, I was able to attend the same intermediate and high school. It wasn't that my family stopped moving, it was that I was determined to keep my same friends and graduate with them. I wrote letters to Boards of Education when we moved explaining why I needed to stay in the same school. I rode my bike, walked, and eventually drove a motorcycle eight miles from a nearby town to stay at La Mirada High School for all four years.

Three particular teachers took a special interest in me and advocated for me throughout high school. They were examples of those rare individuals who see what is not told or shared. Mr. Burns encouraged me to apply for Honor Society at a time when I had lost belief in myself. When I voiced my insecurities, he mirrored back my accomplishments and told me he would assure I became a member. After a particularly bad incident in which I broke the law, Mr. Hadley volunteered as a character witness for me and helped me work through the legal issue. Mr. Saucedo counseled me and encouraged college.

Ted Okey with his wife, Merrilee, grandson, Leif Eric Osborn (above), and son, Neil (below).

Early on in life, I formed a philosophy centered around love. I reasoned that to be a happy and fulfilled person one must believe in oneself as both loving and lovable. Further, I believed every life required a balance of love, creative outlets, and work that is fulfilling. Through education and family, I have found this balance.

Building upon strengths and overcoming obstacles and adversity, in short being resilient, is no protection from hardship, setbacks, and relapses. What it does is provide a language and a set of tools and experiences to rely on when the going gets tough.

At age 18, when my parents divorced and both announced that they did not want to know me any further, I entered a period of rebellion, anger, and self-destruction. I credit the memories of 11 years with a loving mother, a positive schooling experience, caring teachers, a belief that my life was meant to make a contribution, and a loving wife and child as the resiliency factors which brought me back to positive answers and to the life I enjoy today. ✳

Ted Okey is principal of Orchard Mesa Middle School in Grand Junction, Colorado. He has also served as the headmaster of a private school and as an assistant superintendent, principal, assistant principal, counselor, teacher, and coach.

Dr. Okey has taught internationally as well as graduate courses for Michigan State University. He has done national presentations and numerous local, state, and regional workshops on dropout prevention. He can be reached at Orchard Mesa Middle School, 2736 C RD, Grand Junction, CO. 81503 • (970)242-5563.

Hell-o Morning, I'm the Principal

5:30, when the alarm rings, I put my feet upon the floor.
My sleep disturbed, I leave the bed, wishing there was more.
I stumble to the bathroom, scratching here and there, and
Rub my eyes to clear the sleep, then straighten down my hair.

I don't know yet that little Joni's cheek is red and bruised.
She called stepdad a jerk last night, and now she's been abused.
I don't know yet that Nora's mom will pull her out of school.
She likes a boy, that's her crime, she broke her parent's rule.

Lowering my head over the sink, I splash cold water on my face,
Then lift the Norelco, turn it on, and it cuts the whiskers at their base.
I climb into my terry robe and feel my way to the bedroom door,
And call Mariah, the golden pup. We take the stairs to the first floor.

I don't know yet that J. J. will be drinking screwdrivers in the hall.
Or that his mom will throw a fit when I have to make that call.
I don't know yet that the wall has been tagged by the Southside Blue,
Or that townfolks will deny there's gangs, when I tell them it is true.

I shut off the house alarm, let out the dog and feed the cat,
Turn on Mr. Coffee, wind the grandfather clock, and pick up this and that.
The first cup from the fresh grounds flavored with raspberries and cream
Clears the cobwebs and erases what was left of last night's dream.

I don't know yet that my bulletin quoting Sizer's essential skills
Has upset the staff and has one science teacher back on ulcer pills.
I don't know yet that a grievance has been filed over the harassment case,
Or that the superintendent will call: This better not blow up in his face.

The strong stream from the hot shower loosens up the stiffness in my neck.
I dress in the dark, splash on cologne, and finish coffee on the deck.
Then comes the morning ritual of filling pockets with keys and wallet and comb.
I take one last look around, kiss my sleeping wife, and say goodbye to home.

I don't know yet that Sandy's dad will hit two kids riding bikes on Cherry Lane,
Or that Mickey is in the psych ward because his mom says he's insane.
I don't know yet the union-elected Board candidate will be stopping by,
Or that a reporter from *The Sentinel* will call asking who, what, and why.

Hell-o morning, I'm the principal and today will be like every other day.
I don't do it for fame or glory. The reward is certainly not in the pay.
I don't know the problems I will face today or what my efforts will be worth.
But I smile as I go to school, for mine is the noblest profession on earth.

—Ted Okey

PART TWO

The Power of Service
and
Adventure Learning

KIDS Consortium Turns Communities Into Classrooms

by Nan Henderson, M.S.W.

"We need to think of kids as problem solvers, not as problems to be solved," says Marvin Rosenblum, executive director and cofounder of KIDS (Kids Involved Doing Service) Consortium, located in South Portland, Maine. "Kids are municipal resources," Rosenblum adds. Communities have always "planned for them, never with them."

Rosenblum founded KIDS in 1991 when, as a planner in the Maine Office of Economic and Community Development, he noticed the absence of young people in community planning processes. Since that time, more than 5,000 young people, starting in Maine and then expanding to Vermont, New Hampshire, Connecticut, and Colorado have been involved in KIDS Consortium projects. The "Kids as Planners" program initiated by KIDS Consortium was just selected from among 178 entries as the recipient of the 1996 National Planning Award for Public Education given by the American Planning Association.

A recently published evaluation of the KIDS Consortium's approach to using kids as resources, conducted by the Edmund S. Muskie Institute of Public Affairs at the University

> *"We need to think of kids as problem solvers, not as problems to be solved... Kids are municipal resources."*

of Southern Maine (see pp.37-39 for additional details), concluded that KIDS Consortium successfully accomplishes its four goals for young people. These are 1) fostering a caring and supportive academic climate which will enhance personal and scholastic achievements; 2) building resiliency and prevention factors in youth; 3) promoting a sense of stewardship for schools and communities among students; and 4) promoting academic achievement among school aged children and youth. The evaluators wrote that as a team, they

> consider the findings [of the evaluation] to be outstanding for a program which is still in its infancy. Perhaps the most exciting is the capacity for the model to enhance resiliency within young people. The program is helping to create empowered teachers and students who will be ready to face the challenges which await us in the coming century. It is also helping to build problem solvers who are learning how to tackle real-world issues and to define real-world needs.... Evidence indicates this model, which is at once exciting and significant, is likely to gain prominence within the changing American education landscape.

KIDS Consortium utilizes several activities to accomplish its goals: networking in communities to enlist the support of all community stakeholders for the KIDS process; hosting workshops for educators and community leaders to demonstrate how the model can be implemented in their communities; providing technical assistance to schools and communities; and promoting the KIDS model and projects through producing a newsletter and videos and engaging in other public relations activities.

KIDS Consortium projects are currently in place in dozens of school districts and communities, including the following:

- **Bath, Maine**: Students at Morse High School are conducting a feasibility study to determine whether the city should offer more recreational opportunities, particularly for its young people. Students are administering a citywide survey, compiling and analyzing data, and creating products to demonstrate the results to the Bath City Council. At Bath Middle School, students are working with the city to renovate the McMann Field complex. Peer leaders organize classes in the design and completion of tasks that move the project forward, from soil sampling to painting and fund raising.
- **Moretown, Vermont**: Students at Moretown Elementary and Harwood High School served as the core team to guide the district's seven schools and six towns in the KIDS process. Students surveyed the citizens of the region, collecting a total of 400 completed survey instruments, in an effort to determine top needs and issues among the citizenry. Recreation, quality of life issues for the elderly, and enhancing the business community emerged. Moretown students developed an open space plan to maximize the recreational use of 150 acres surrounding the elementary school. Activities included researching property boundaries, coordinating with local officials and the media, tree planting, and extensive trail mapping. All subject areas were utilized in this process.

> *"Perhaps the most exciting is the capacity for the model to enhance resiliency within young people."*

- **Orono (Maine) High School**: Every student learns about community problems and issues and then develops and implements a personal Service Learning Action Plan. Recently, school chemistry classes worked with the pharmacy at Eastern Maine Medical Center to conduct a retrospective study on morbidity of nausea in cardiac surgery patients; technology classes constructed bat houses for the Page Farm and Home Museum; applied math classes conducted trash audits; and physical science classes continued to help elderly residents compost in preparation for a spring garden.
- **Portland, Maine**: With funding from the Casco Bay Estuary Project, middle school and high school students from Lincoln Middle School, King Middle School, and Deering High School have been developing a monitoring

program for the Fore River Estuary. In addition to collecting data on water quality, students are working through interdisciplinary teams and independent study to research issues related to human impact on the bay, such as clam flat closures and nonpoint source pollution. Through their findings, students are making recommendations on actions that parents and fellow classmates can take to become more responsible stewards of the bay.

- **Jay (Maine) High School**: With the support of International Paper, students are designing River Walk, a multi-use recreational trail and park along the Androscoggin River.
- **Wells (Maine) Elementary School**: Third and fourth graders opened the "Kids's Korner Store" in their school. Students staff the store, make change, stock inventory, place orders, and keep handwritten tallies and records of each sale. Before the store opened, the students surveyed their peers about items to sell, named the business, designed a logo, and outlined jobs. They examined the local stores to set prices and marketed their store through designing, printing, and distributing fliers. The store now averages $200 a week, and the students decide what to do with their 15 to 20% profit.

> *"Prevention just happens as kids feel good and potent."*

- **Manchester, New Hampshire**: A second grade class at Parker-Varney Elementary School has been working to create a "Big Book" of the school's history in honor of the school's 25th anniversary. At Manchester High School West, students led a half-day orientation session for over 100 incoming freshmen. The older students organized all facets of the orientation, from planning to serving as tour guides for new students.

"I feel proud to actually take part in something this important," commented Keyonna Scott about her participation as a sixth grader in a KIDS project in Lewiston, Maine where she and her classmates revitalized a local pond. "They usually have scientists working on something like this," she added. Rosenblum reports that her comment is typical of student reactions. "Kids need to share in a process that allows them to recognize and experience their own power," he says. He notes that KIDS was not started as a prevention program, though it is now clear to him that this is what it accomplishes. "Prevention just happens as kids feel good and potent." ✳

KIDS Consortium is funded through private and public contributions. For more information about KIDS, write or call them at 45 Bridgton Road, Westbrook, ME 04092, (207)878-6270.

The following profile of the KIDS Consortium ELF Woods Project is reprinted by permission from the Spring, 1995 issue of Voices of Change, *a publication of the Maine Center for Educational Services in Auburn, Maine. The journal was funded by a grant from the Pugh Charitable Trust.*

Sharing the Power: The ELF Woods Project Taps the Energy and Talents of Students as They Improve Their Community

The "snake trail" was a winding, eroded tar path, east of Edward Little High School in Auburn, Maine, neglected, littered, and notorious as a hangout for truants and troublemakers. In the fall of 1992 Brian Flynn, an English teacher, challenged his students to a simple writing assignment: "What would you do to improve the snake trail?" At first, students dreamed up impossible ideas—a water slide, castle, chair lift, flame throwing lights—and then some practical ones—a gazebo, pond, campground, trail system.... As students grew excited about the possibilities, they began to insist, "Instead of just talking about fixing up the area, why don't we actually do something?"

Since that time, over 300 students have been involved in designing and implementing a 50-page master plan to transform 40 acres of wilderness into a place that is safe, aesthetically pleasing, environmentally sound, and enjoyable for students and community residents alike. The master plan outlines the purpose, benefit, necessary modifications, term for completion, cost, and required manpower for the following six recommendations:

- 400-yard walkway resurfaced with asphalt and accented with cobblestone;
- Lights to facilitate evening commutes;
- Landscaping including picnic tables, benches, trash receptacles, and signs;
- Mountain biking trail with switchbacks and berms;
- Cross country trail for competitive athletic use;
- Obstacle course, complete with walls, tire swings, ropes, cargo net, and rocks.

The Model

The ELF (Edward Little Franklin) Woods Project is one of dozens fostered by the KIDS (Kids Involved Doing Service) Consortium, a 501(c)(3) private, nonprofit organization. KIDS as Planners is an innovative educational process [facilitated by KIDS Consortium] which engages students in working to solve real-life problems in their communities as part of math, science, English, social studies, and other subjects. In addition to land-use planning, students of all ages in over 50 towns across New England are protecting wildlife, preserving cultural artifacts, documenting local history, assessing public health, cleaning up rivers and ponds, designing parks and playgrounds, and generally "getting involved" in making a difference, not as a "nice" activity, but as an integral part of comprehensive planning and educational reform efforts.

> *"Through the ELF Woods Project, students have been able to develop and apply a variety of talents including linguistic, logical, spatial, artistic, interpersonal, and leadership abilities."*

The process directly addresses academic failure and lack of social bonding, the risk factors most common to substance abuse, juvenile delinquency, teen pregnancy, suicide, school dropout, and other destructive behaviors. In fact, research has shown that opportunities for young people to participate in the life of the community enables them to develop problem-solving abilities, social competence, autonomy, and a sense of hope and future—attributes that enable them to "bounce back" from "at risk" environments.

The Town as the Classroom

Auburn sits on the Androscoggin River which, 20 years ago, provided lifeblood to dozens of shoe and textile manufacturing companies. But today, unemployment stands at 9%. The changes within the community are leading to changes in its schools. Over the past two years, a design team comprised of school and community members has been developing a strategic plan to restructure education in the Auburn school system "so that all students learn and succeed in a changing world."

The ELF Woods Project is the manifestation of this bold new approach to education. While English classes are still responsible for reading literature, building vocabulary, and writing journals and book reports, the City of Auburn has become the "test" for learning and applying these skills in a real-world context. In addition to writing, revising, and editing the master plan, students are involved in the following activities:

- Research, from conducting a site analysis to plot topography, wildlife, vegetation, water flow, and other natural features to investigating present and desired uses of the property through interviews with students and community residents and an analysis of historical records;
- Public speaking, from debate and consensus-making with fellow students to negotiation with city officials and formal presentations to the student body, school board, city council, civic organizations, and national audiences;

- Using technology to design maps, illustrations, charts, and timelines to effectively communicate the desired vision;
- Teaching, from producing television and film clips to apprenticing younger students and facilitating groups of teachers to help them plan community projects.

In order to balance the demands of content and process, teachers must establish parameters within which students can share the power and take responsibility for their own learning. Ultimately, "sharing the power" works both ways. When a teacher empowers students to make decisions about their own learning, they, in turn, must be willing to share their talents with the group. Through the ELF Woods Project, students have been able to develop and apply a variety of talents including linguistic, logical, spatial, artistic, interpersonal, and leadership abilities. Greg Lavertu, class of '94, admits that he was classified as an "at risk" student, "which means I wasn't supposed to get this far." But the experience helped him grow, and now, as a student at Unity College and a member of the Maine Conservation Corps, he recognizes that "everybody has something to offer, and it's our duty as intellects and human beings to take what that person has to offer." Sharing the power is the process that values student abilities and demands student performance.

Apprentice Citizenship

"If we are to apprentice young people as citizens of a democratic society, educators must value the application of knowledge over the mere acquisition of knowledge," asserts Marvin Rosenblum, executive director of the KIDS Consortium. "Every kid deserves the opportunity to make a difference." Indeed, what makes KIDS as Planners different from other "project-based," "hands-on," and experiential learning methodologies is that students take action. Josh Stevens, a junior, explains, "Without approval, the master plan would have been just a 50-page plan sitting on a shelf somewhere." Instead, the students set up a referendum and brought it to the student body at Edward Little. The outcome? Over 360 students voted in favor, with only 59 opposed—a resounding six to one ratio.

> *"If we are to apprentice young people as citizens of a democratic society, educators must value the application of knowledge over the mere acquisition of knowledge."*

From there, students presented the plan to the school board and then to the city council, finally negotiating a $15,000 Community Development Block Grant to implement the plan. To date, students have raised over $34,000 with help from 30 public and private agencies, including International Paper, Maine Community Foundation, Geiger Bros., General Electric, and Project SEED. Public officials and private citizens have also served as important resources. Lee Jay Feldman, Auburn city planner, helped students develop the master plan. John Footer, a local stone mason, helped students harvest cobblestones. Specialists from the Soil and Water Conservation District certified control measures. A professional surveyor assisted students in plotting the features of the obstacle course. Currently, students are negotiating with General Durgan of the Air Force National Guard to provide about $80,000 worth of cable for the lights.

This kind of personal achievement is both public and permanent. "When students accept challenges and act on them, their success is what really builds self esteem," reflects Alumni Allen Campbell. There is no substitute for creating something with your own mind, writing something with your own pen, or building something with your own two hands. Ironically, students have said that it is not what other people do for them that gives them confidence and strength, but what they do for themselves and what they do for other people in their community. Most of the time you will find that they have just never been asked.

Critical Mass

Last year, the KIDS Concortium trained over 600 people in the KIDS model. By bringing together educators, preventionists, public officials, business leaders, and community members to explore their own town as a classroom, KIDS workshops serve as catalysts to help schools break free of the "special project" design that plagues so many educational innovations. They also help create a critical mass of people willing to work together to structure and sustain learning opportunities that empower young people.

> *"Ironically, students have said that it is not what other people do for them that gives them confidence and strength, but what they do for themselves and what they do for other people in their community."*

At Edward Little, for example, the ELF Woods Project has fostered interdisciplinary learning. Pam Buffington, a computer technology teacher, helped students generate professional reports and products for the project. With the help of science teacher Margaret Wilson, students created scientific extracts to document flora and fauna native to the woods. This year, as a spinoff to the ELF Woods project, students in Tina Vanasse's geometry classes are designing and building a greenhouse that will operate as a student-run business.

Students are not problems to be solved but priceless resources with talent and energy. Likewise, teachers are not repositories of information but guides and facilitators for student learning. "Mr. Flynn looked to us for answers as much, if not more, than we did to him," reflects Greg Lavertu. When, at last, schools, towns, businesses, and community-based organizations can share the power of their talents and expertise, we can create learning that empowers and education that matters. ⁂

KIDS Beautify Norwich's Heritage Walkway
by the Norwich Connecticut Schools' Third Grade Classes

One day we were studying social studies. We talked about our community and what was fun in Norwich. One of the places we mentioned was Heritage Walkway. It is a 1.4 mile walkway that starts at the marina and ends at the old powerhouse on the Yantic River. We noticed that the walk was very dirty. People treated it like a trash can. We wanted to clean it up. It is important to all of us that nature is clean.

We made a plan to pick up trash, to plant flowers, and to put up some birdhouses. We listed all the things we needed to do the job. Then we listed the materials and the equipment we would need. Then we asked ourselves what steps would be needed. Then we put the steps in order. We thought of possible problems. Once we were done doing that we thought of the solutions for all of them.

We wrote a letter to Ms. Bram-Mereen, the assistant city planner, and asked if the third grade classes and Mrs. Mercier's kindergarten class could help clean it up. She sent a letter back saying we could help out on the city's Earth Day Cleanup. We invited her to come to talk to us about it. She gave us maps and told us that after the cleanup we would all have pizza and soda. She also gave our school a banner for taking part in the cleanup.

On Saturday, April 20, parents helped us to clean up. Ms. Bram-Mereen took care of the garbage cans and bags. We took care of the gloves. We worked hard for two hours. Ms. Bram-Mereen gave us little rose patches to thank us for helping.

We chose to plant flowers at a place near the power house. So far we have tested the soil for its pH level, worked the soil to remove grass and weeds, and planted some day lilies. Pretty soon we will plant more flowers. Then we will put up some bird houses that our families have made and sent in.

We Learned a Few Things, Too

Many varied and unusual things that we've learned along
the way during our Heritage Walkway Project are:

- letter writing
- telephone manners
- making graphs
- writing math story problems
- testing soil for the pH level
- what perennials and annuals are
- estimating how long it takes to walk a mile
- estimating area
- estimating perimeter
- measuring area & perimeter
- measuring distances
- dividing tools among groups
- planning projects
- making decisions
- drawing murals
- working in groups
- writing summaries
- adding details to paragraphs
- using the computer to write
- drawing on the computer
- making a computer report about our project
- talking to people who can help us learn about our community
- helping our community is fun
- planting seeds and watching them grow
- learning what plants need to grow
- how birds like their own space

Reprinted with permission from the KIDS Consortium Newsletter

KIDS in Action and Other Service Learning Programs Produce Results

by Bonnie Benard, M.S.W.

The University of Southern Maine did an initial evaluation of the KIDS Consortium KIDSNET project, finding positive effects on school attendance, grades, problem solving, and stewardship. A further evaluation is planned to also look at the impact of the KIDS approach on self-esteem, substance use, violence, and youth attitudes toward communities. Loren Coleman, Project Leader of the KIDS evaluation, notes:

> The University of Southern Maine's evaluative findings demonstrated the value of the KIDS model as a teaching tool and as a methodology for promoting resiliency in youth. Attempts to measure such outcomes have not occurred in the past, and we were pleased with the initial results gathered. There is a need for further study and evaluations in more detail, chronologically followed for a longer period of time. The implications of the KIDS model are significant, and the more data collected about it the better. (p. 15)

An interim evaluation of Learn and Serve programs nationally (Brandeis University & Abt Associates, 1996) has shown the power of service learning to effect not only individual outcomes but also to positively impact cooperating schools and community organizations, as well as the larger community.

Service Learning Impacts Students and Improves Community Organizations

Service learning programs showed statistically significant, positive impacts on several measures of civic and educational development, including:

- engagement in school
- personal responsibility
- grades
- social responsibility
- core subject GPA
- acceptance of cultural diversity
- educational aspirations
- leadership

During the 1995-96 school year, Learn and Serve students were involved in more than 300 district projects or activities in each semester, providing more than 154,000 hours of service over the year. Officials of community organizations consistently gave students high praise for the "valued additions" they provided to their organizations' mission and work.

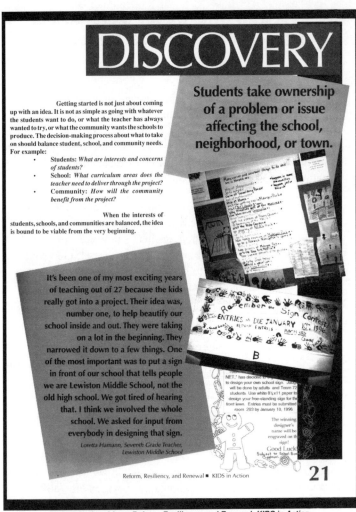

DISCOVERY

Getting started is not just about coming up with an idea. It is not as simple as going with whatever the students want to do, or what the teacher has always wanted to try, or what the community wants the schools to produce. The decision-making process about what to take on should balance student, school, and community needs. For example:

- Students: *What are interests and concerns of students?*
- School: *What curriculum areas does the teacher need to deliver through the project?*
- Community: *How will the community benefit from the project?*

When the interests of students, schools, and communities are balanced, the idea is bound to be viable from the very beginning.

Students take ownership of a problem or issue affecting the school, neighborhood, or town.

It's been one of my most exciting years of teaching out of 27 because the kids really got into a project. Their idea was, number one, to help beautify our school inside and out. They were taking on a lot in the beginning. They narrowed it down to a few things. One of the most important was to put a sign in front of our school that tells people we are Lewiston Middle School, not the old high school. We got tired of hearing that. I think we involved the whole school. We asked for input from everybody in designing that sign.

Loretta Hamann, Seventh Grade Teacher, Lewiston Middle School

B

Reform, Resiliency, and Renewal ■ KIDS in Action

21

A page reprinted from *Reform, Resilience, and Renewal: KIDS in Action*, a guidebook to their program published by KIDS Consortium.

On a 10-point scale (with 10 as "best possible"), the officials' ratings for the student participants averaged:

- 8.7 for their impact on clients
- 8.2 for their community impact

In addition, 96% of the officials polled said they would use the student volunteers again; 75% said that the volunteers had helped raise the skill levels, engagement, and self-esteem of their clients; and over 66% said that the volunteers had fostered a more *positive attitude toward working with the schools*, with over 50% stating that new relationships with the public schools had been produced.

The KIDS Model and Key Components of Effective Service Learning

In an earlier study of service learning commissioned by the Carnegie Foundation (Harrington & Schine, 1989), researchers identified the key components of successful service learning as:

- Staff *believes* that youth are resources.
- Students make real decisions and solve real problems.
- Responsibilities and accountability are clear.
- Classroom learning occurs in authentic ways.
- Teachers and adults involved are nurturing (an essential component).
- Time for processing, planning, and reflection on service is provided for both students *and* teachers.

It is clear that KIDS is a model that absolutely does all of these, and more. I encourage everyone who cares about children and youth to experience and enjoy *Reform, Resiliency, and Renewal: KIDS in Action*. It offers hope and guidance to all concerned with rebuilding communities. ❋

References

Brandeis University & Abt Associates (1996). *National evaluation of Learn and Serve America school and community-based programs: Interim report.* Washington, D.C.: Corporation for National Service.

Harrington, D., & Schine, J. (1989). *Connections: Service learning in the middle grades.* New York: Carnegie Corporation.

Lappe, F.M., & DuBois, P.M. (1994). *The quickening of America: Re-building our nation, remaking our lives.* San Francisco: Jossey-Bass.

Reform, Resiliency, and Renewal: KIDS in Action

KIDS Consortium,
45 Bridgton Road,
Westbrook, Maine 04092

- (207-878-6270)

Paperback, 103 pages
- $14.95 (plus $4.00 s/h)

L.W. Schmick:
Challenging the "At Risk" Label

by Nan Henderson, M.S.W.

The drop out prevention, resiliency, and youth treatment literature is filled with research evidence about the detrimental impact of negatively labeling young people, adults, families, and communities. This literature is also rich with reports of how a single person or opportunity can turn around the life of a person, family, or community so labeled. L.W. Schmick's story personalizes this research. His wisdom, shared below, reiterates how labels do the opposite of helping, and how, in Bonnie Benard's words, resiliency is often the result of "one person or one opportunity or one caring family member, teacher, or friend, who encouraged a child's success and welcomed his or her participation."

When L.W. Schmick was in middle school, he realized he was in a class that "was different" from other kids. By his freshman year in high school, he knew that his classes were for "at risk" students. Though he says he "wasn't ever mad at teachers for seeing that and being aware of that," he thinks the label was detrimental to himself and his peers.

"Putting an 'at risk' student in a separate class just separates them more. And I think that's what a lot of "at risk" students are trying not to do [be more separate]. I think they should be blended in more so they are not put in their own little group," L.W. explained.

> **"One of the results of being labeled, he said, is that students feel since they've already been labeled, why even try."**

One of the results of being labeled, he said, is that students feel since they've already been labeled, why even try. He used to say to himself, "It doesn't matter. I'll be 'at risk.' No big deal." He added, "It just seemed like everyone was waiting, watching for us to fail." He and his peers felt that all their behaviors were "under a magnifying glass."

L.W. was labeled "at risk" after he got into "a lot" of trouble in fifth and sixth grade. He and his mother had just moved to Maine from New York State, and for him the move "was a big deal." He had to leave his entire family behind, including his father who had been divorced from his mother when L.W. was only six months old, but who was still an important person in his life. His reaction to the move: "I was big for my age, so I had older friends around. I got in a lot of fights. I got in trouble at school, and I didn't get along with teachers very well." L.W. got suspended from school in sixth grade.

He says that in looking back at that time, he realized one of the major reasons he got into so much trouble was "I just wanted to fit in... and it is pretty hard to fit in when you're a six foot red head. Blending into a crowd isn't the easiest thing to do." This is one reason he feels that being separated in middle school into a class for tough kids only made things worse. He was thrown off the middle school basketball team "for being mean," he received a lot of detention, and he started drinking.

L.W. credits his parents with providing him with some of what helped turn his life around. He said he always felt unconditional love and support from both of them. His mom stopped working two jobs so she could be home when he got home from school. His dad encouraged him to find a vocation in life, which meant staying in school. And L.W. himself said he never seriously considered dropping out of school because he realized that would "be quitting and I don't like to quit."

L.W. Schmick: "Just another person: Not an 'at risk' student."

His life began to change his freshman year in high school when he was forced to find new friends (who were more connected to school) because "all my other friends dropped out." In fact, only 2 of the 15 students in his "at risk" middle school class—the class "no one really wanted to mess with, the class for 'the bad kids'"—graduated from high school. L.W. was one of the two. And he graduated with the respect of his teachers, his peers, and his community thanks to a KIDS Consortium trained teacher (see previous chapter on KIDS Consortium) to whom L.W. gives most of the credit. L.W. said it is because of this teacher and the opportunity this teacher offered to become involved in a KIDS Consortium Project that he is headed this fall to college to become a teacher himself.

"In my sophomore year, I had an English class with Brian Flynn," who started the ELF Woods Project (see pp. 32-36). "A lot of teachers when they see an 'at risk' student, they automatically distrust and they don't give them some of the responsibilities they would give other students... because they're 'at risk' supposedly," L.W. said. But Brian Flynn "showed me respect and trust. He gave me a lot of power to take responsibility. He said, 'If you want an inch, take an inch. If you want a mile, take a mile.'" And, he added, in Brian's class, "I wasn't set apart as different. I was able to mix in. He saw me as just another person, not as an 'at risk' student."

When asked what else about Brian Flynn was so different than other teachers he had previously had, L.W. added: "[Most] teachers see students as students and they're above you when they're teaching you and you listen to what they say because that's what is right. But Brian took a lot of what the students had to say, and that's how we did a lot of the things in the class. Someone would say 'it would be better like this,' so we'd try it like that. He shared his power with us."

After his experience in Brian's class, and working on the ELF Woods Project, L.W. said he became more involved with his community. And he gained more respect for community, "for all the hard work that it takes to do some things." The experience of having some of his work in the ELF Woods Project vandalized also taught L.W. "how people hurt when you destroy their things."

> *"A lot of teachers when they see an 'at risk' student, they automatically distrust and they don't give them some of the responsibilities they would give other students... because they're 'at risk' supposedly."*

After his sophomore year L.W. stayed involved. He worked with the local National Guard to put lights along a trail behind his school. He worked with General Electric to get all the equipment and with the city of Auburn to get the permits.

After his work with the Elf Woods Project, and his continuing service in his junior and senior years, L.W. said, "That 'at risk' label had been erased. I liked school more." Other people saw him differently, he said, and when this happened, "then I changed."

His advice to teachers dealing with difficult students: "I can see how teachers would be a little weary of an 'at risk' student. But it doesn't necessarily mean that we're dumb or that 'at risk' [students] are less able to do things, it just means that sometimes for circumstances beyond their control they're 'at risk.' Which was my case, I think. So try to treat us like you treat everyone else." ❋

Nan Henderson, M.S.W., is a national speaker and consultant on fostering resiliency and wellness, alcohol and other drug issues, and on organizational change. She has co-authored/edited five books about resiliency, and is the Editor-in-chief at Resiliency In Action, Inc. She can be reached at Nan Henderson and Associates, 5130 La Jolla Blvd., #2K, San Diego, CA 92109, p/f (858-488-5034), or by e-mail: (nanh@connectnet.com).

Adventures in Resiliency: The Power of Adventure Learning

by Helen Beatie, Ed.D.

Adventure learning is a powerful teaching paradigm which provides a framework to promote resiliency in the school setting. The marriage of resiliency theory and adventure learning is explored in this article, linking the six key protective conditions defined by Henderson and Milstein (1996) with the essential elements of adventure learning. (These conditions are explained in chapters one and two.)

What is Adventure Learning?

Think back a moment to your most memorable learning experience—that time in your life when a passion for discovery or some new or different understanding of your world was sparked. What were the attributes of this experience? When a group of 25 fourth through 12th graders were challenged with this question, they arrived at the following key elements: helping relationships, action, challenge, discovery, creativity, and enjoyment. When a group of adults shared some examples of this moment, their choices ranged from an elementary school field trip to Fort Ticonderoga, New York, where history suddenly came alive, to the mystery of the transformation of simple batter into a cream puff. From moments such as these are born life-long passions.

> *"Adventure learning practitioners seek to sustain and foster that childhood thirst for learning, which is all too often lost as young people progress through our educational institutions."*

Think also of the creative play of a young child, a natural and unparalleled vehicle for growth. It is comprised of an endless series of joyous discoveries, ranging from the relentless quest of an eight-month-old to experience the world from his full height, to the first time a five-year-old finds the balance point on her two-wheel bicycle. Curiosity, mingled with an element of real or perceived risk, draws the young child into learning. Whatever one's age, inevitably these life-changing learning experiences contain the essential ingredients of *adventure*.

Adventure learning is inspired by the work of educational philosopher, John Dewey (1938), dating back to the early part of this century. Contemporary influences include Outward Bound and Project Adventure. Dewey contended that individuals learn best through direct experience rather than passive learning. Teachers first immerse students in action, and then ask them to reflect on the experience. Self-discovery, and generalization of the experience through reflection, form the foundation of adventure learning. Adventure learning practitioners seek to sustain and foster that childhood thirst for learning, which is all too often lost as young people progress through our educational institutions (Henton, 1996).

Ropes courses are an increasingly well-known setting for adventure learning. Ropes course activities present novel and challenging problems to an individual or a group. These activities contain an element of risk, offer the opportunity for significant accomplishment, and progressively build trust. They usually include some physical challenge. For example, the group might be asked to move across a "raging, alligator-filled river" via a rope suspended yards beyond reach of any participant, or to fall backwards into the arms of peers

> *"Adventure learning also instills an understanding of social responsibility, allowing participants to experience the rewards of giving of oneself for the larger good, while learning to respect and value human diversity."*

from a height of five feet. Importantly, experiences in this controlled learning environment serve as a metaphor for life situations: *The process of decision making and task accomplishment is the ultimate measure of success, rather than mere completion of the challenge.*

Adventure-based activities, whether on the ropes course or in the classroom, provide a learning laboratory to explore individual and group decision making, leadership qualities, the power of cooperation, the richness of diversity, and communication skills. This approach has been shown to heighten self-confidence, facilitate group and personal growth, improve problem-solving skills, and promote more effective team work (Braverman, Brenner, Fretz, & Desmond, 1990; Bronson, Gibson, Kichar, & Priest, 1992; Hart & Kilka, 1994; Priest, 1996; Priest & Gass, 1997; Shoel, Prouty, & Radcliffe, 1988; Rohnke, 1989). As discussed below, increased resiliency is another potential outcome.

Vermont's Orleans Southwest Supervisory Union (OSSU) built a low ropes course as a means to introduce adventure learning into its six schools three years ago. Since that time, many teachers, having successfully completed a facilitator training course, have brought their students to the low ropes course and adventure into their classrooms. They have integrated adventure learning principles with the strengths-based resiliency paradigm, and achieved impressive results.

A discussion of how the key attributes of adventure learning support the six fundamental protective factors which build resiliency in young people follows. Quotes from the OSSU student evaluations following a ropes course experience are offered as anecdotal evidence of the power of adventure learning as a vehicle for supporting healthy youth development.

Resiliency Theory as a Basis for Adventure Learning

Teach Life Skills

Adventure learning involves communication, problem solving, conflict resolution, and leadership skill development. Adventure learning also instills an understanding of social responsibility, allowing participants to experience the rewards of giving of oneself for the larger good, while learning to respect and value human diversity. These are all fundamental life skills.

Student reflections when asked what they learned included:

"I learned good communication skills, but most important to listen to others." —eleventh grader

"Cooperation and teamwork." —all grades

"Anger management." —eighth grader

"One thing I learned was to not put-down so much—to look at people differently and not with one view." —eleventh grader

Increase Prosocial Bonding

The sequence of adventure learning activities are carefully constructed to assure that participants gain increasing degrees of trust, thereby creating physical and emotional safety. Each group defines social norms, including such key reassurances as "no put-downs of self or others" and "honoring differences." Tasks require cooperation to be accomplished. The atmosphere of trust and respect which groups develop often stands in stark contrast to the students' school and home environments, and so provides a powerful opportunity for individuals to bond with peers.

Student reflections when asked what they learned included:

"If I need to talk to someone in school, I know I can trust them and they can trust me." —sixth grader

"I learned a lot about different people that I probably would have never come into contact with." —eleventh grader

Set Clear and Consistent Boundaries

One fundamental tool for adventure learning is called the Full Value Commitment (FVC). This is a behavioral agreement defined and agreed to by all participants. It gives students control and ownership of their learning environment. Students are asked to first identify all the qualities they want as attributes of their time together. Each person's suggestion is written down after the group has reached a mutual understanding about the

> *"By actively engaging students in setting clear and consistent behavioral guidelines for their adventure learning or school experience, many of the behavioral issues and power struggles prompted by traditional, teacher-centered behavior management models are circumvented."*

meaning of the particular attribute. Because many children do not intuit inappropriate social behavior, participants then identify all those behaviors which could undermine this group vision. Next, all students sign their work, signifying their agreement and commitment to follow the FVC to the best of their abilities. The final step entails the development of consequences if the terms of the FVC are not followed.

Many classroom teachers in the OSSU now begin the year with this exercise and frequently refer back to the FVC to help the class identify their strengths and areas of desired change. Students add or delete attributes as the group deems appropriate. By actively engaging students in setting clear and consistent behavioral guidelines for their adventure learning or school experience, many of the behavioral issues and power struggles prompted by traditional, teacher-centered behavior management models are circumvented.

"In an atmosphere of trust and respect, the human spirit is free to grow. Strengths are brought forth and the basic goodness of all individuals is abundantly evident."

Seventh-grade student reflections on the most meaningful aspect of the Full Value Commitment included:

"Makes me feel safe and wanting to come to school."

"Hope and trust."

"That we all signed it and have to obey it and that we all made some contribution."

Provide Caring and Support

Trust becomes the foundation for a nurturing environment. The noncompetitive premise for all activities and continual focus on cooperation leads to genuine and deep relationships amongst participants and between participants and the teacher or facilitator. Caring and support are invariably key attributes identified in the FVC. Furthermore, the FVC process provides group members with the opportunity to define these terms to their own satisfaction (i.e., provide encouragement, protect the physical safety of others, etc.).

Participants experience caring and support physically as well as emotionally within adventure activities. For example, choosing to fall into the arms of your group is often a powerful reminder of one's need for unequivocal trust and support. Participants gain more than an intellectual understanding of their importance to the group; they also form strong and enduring visceral memories of caring and reassurance.

One ninth-grade student reflected on what she learned:

"When you are up in the air, people believe that you can do whatever you put your mind to, because I heard people saying, 'Come on, you can do it.' [Every person] thought, 'I can do it, I can!' and that makes you feel great inside."

Provide Opportunities for Meaningful Participation

The cooperative nature of all activities continually reinforces the importance of the participation of each person in the group. The novel tasks also draw upon a wide array of skills and abilities, engaging participants in varied ways. For this reason, adventure learning activities offer nontraditional learners (often more nonverbal or hands-on learners) a unique opportunity to demonstrate their capabilities, reaffirming their skills and worth. Although the contrived nature of ropes courses may not at first glance seem meaningful (as pointed out by a number of skeptics who ponder the value of "swinging from the trees"), the metaphors which are continually drawn to both school and home life by the adventure learning facilitators are undeniably important.

> **"Schools which have fully integrated adventure learning principles into all aspects of the education process are experiencing dramatic positive academic results."**

Adventure learning in the classroom often takes on the form of thematic, multidisciplinary units utilizing cooperative learning strategies (Henton, 1996; Horwood, 1995; Sakofs & Armstrong, 1996). These teaching strategies draw in students who might otherwise feel removed and distant from the learning process, assuring that a greater number of students are meaningfully involved in their school experience.

One eleventh-grade student reflected on what she learned:

"I learned that every person has something to contribute to the team, no matter what grade or age."

Set and Communicate High Expectations

Adventure learning is comprised of novel and highly challenging activities. In many instances both individuals and groups harbor grave doubts about their ability to accomplish an activity. However, appropriate sequencing of challenges generally assures that the group will have a high probability of task completion. Furthermore, individual and group goal setting is basic to the adventure experience, reinforcing the individual's capacity to set and meet high standards. In this way, high expectations are internalized and participants learn to never assume that the seemingly impossible is in fact out of reach.

Student reflections on what they learned included:

"You can do anything by making plans or goals." —third grader

"When I thought I couldn't do it, they (classmates) said I could and I did." —ninth grader

"I did it to prove that I could, and to know for myself, I did that, and I can get through other obstacles in my life." —tenth grader

"That challenging yourself is fun." —third grader

Adventure Learning Within the School Setting

Adventure learning is being integrated into public school curricula throughout the country. It serves both as a prevention medium and as an intervention tool. For example, Vermont's OSSU has integrated adventure learning into the following aspects of education over the course of the last three years: 1) a three-day sixth to seventh grade transition program, 2) a year-long middle school adventure learning unit, 3) use of the low ropes course by students, staff, and board members, 4) a family ropes course day, 5) an adventure-based counseling program for elementary school students who engage in challenging behaviors in the classroom, 6) an "Adventures in Leadership" elective course for ninth through 12th graders, 7) a core component of guidance and physical education programs, and 8) widespread use of the Full Value Commitment as a classroom behavior management strategy. The adventure learning program continues to grow as teachers witness the learning potential of this medium and the joy of discovery which it sparks in their students. Schools which have fully integrated adventure learning principles into all aspects of the education process are experiencing dramatic positive academic results (Terry & Glasbrenner, 1996).

Adventure Learning as Educational Reform

Adventure learning is based on the assumption that all individuals are "at-promise" and provides a powerful medium in which to identify and explore their gifts. The adventure learning pedagogy assumes a diversity of learning styles, honors multiple intelligences, and teaches essential social and problem-solving skills. It is founded on team development and cooperation rather than competition, fostering strong intrinsic standards and motivation. High expectations are coupled with equally high levels of support and trust. In short, adventure learning is founded upon the basic principles of educational reform embodied in *"These teaching strategies draw in students who might otherwise feel removed and distant from the learning process, assuring that a greater number of students are meaningfully involved in their school experience."* the resiliency theory (Henderson & Milstein, 1996).

Adventure brings people to the far edge of their life experiences and invites them to take one more step beyond what they know. It demands letting go of control and immersing oneself in a new venture. Curiosity outweighs fear; self-doubt is balanced by a calling forth of strengths; and vulnerability takes a back seat to the vision of a greater reward. Through experiences which tap all senses, knowledge grows from within and remains alive long after lectures and textbook lessons are forgotten. In an atmosphere of trust and respect, the human spirit is free to grow. Strengths are brought forth and the basic goodness of all individuals is abundantly evident.

Adventure need not be something which people outgrow as they leave the joyous early childhood years of play and endless intrigue. The inherent resiliency of individuals lives side-by-side with an inherent desire for growth through experience. Adventure learning honors and unites these two fundamental forces, providing a potent vehicle for learning about ourselves and the world around us.

Tell me, and I will forget;
Show me, and I may remember;
Involve me, and I will understand.
—Chinese Proverb

References

Braverman, M., Brenner, J., Fretz, P. & Desmond. D. (1990). Three approaches to evaluation: A ropes course illustration. *Journal of Experiential Education, 13*(1), 23-30.

Bronson, J., Gibson, S., Kichar, R. & Priest, S. (1992). Evaluation of team development in a corporate adventure training program. *Journal of Experiential Education, 15*(2), 50-53.

Dewey, J. (1938). *Experience and education.* New York: Macmillan.

Hart, L., & Silka, L. (1994). Building self-efficacy through women-centered ropes course experiences. In E. Cole; E. Erdman; & E. D. Rothblum (Eds.), *Wilderness therapy for women: The power of adventure,* 111-127.

Henderson, N., & Milstein, M. (1996). *Resiliency in schools: Making it happen for students and educators.* Thousand Oaks, CA: Corwin Press, Inc.

Henton, M. (1996). *Adventure in the classroom.* Dubuque, Iowa: Kendall/Hunt.

Horwood, B. (1995). *Experience and the curriculum.* Dubuque, Iowa: Kendall/Hunt.

Priest, S. (1996). The effect of two different debriefing approaches on developing self-confidence. *Journal of Experiential Education, 19*(1), 40-42.

Priest, S., & Gass, M. (1997). An examination of "problem-solving" versus "solution-focused" facilitation styles in a corporate setting. *Journal of Experiential Education, 20*(1), 34-39.

Rhonke, K. (1989). *Cowstails and cobras II.* Dubuque, Iowa: Kendall/Hunt.

Sakofs, M., & Armstrong, G. (1996). *Into the classroom: The outward bound approach to teaching and learning.* Dubuque, Iowa: Kendall/Hunt.

Shoel, J., Prouty, D., Radcliffe, P. (1988). *Islands of healing: A guide to adventure-based counseling.* Hamilton, MA: Project Adventure, Inc.

Terry, N., & Glasbrenner, M. (Winter, 1996). One of the best schools ever... *Zip Lines, Project Adventure Newsletter,* 31-33.

Helen Beatie, Ed.D., is a school psychologist for Orleans Southwest Supervisory Union in Hardwick, Vermont. She is also an adjunct faculty member at Lyndon State College, Lyndonville, Vermont where she has taught both Adventure-Based Counseling and Ropes Course Facilitator Training courses for the past four years, and presented a number of workshops on this topic.

Adventure Education and Outward Bound Make A Lasting Difference: A Meta-Analysis by John Hattie and Colleagues

by Bonnie Benard, M.S.W.

Adventure Education programs usually involve small groups of students, young and old, who are transported to the wilderness and assigned challenging tasks such as mastering a river rapid or hiking to a remote point (see previous chapter for additional details). The largest is Outward Bound, a private, nonprofit group serving more than 40,000 students worldwide each year. This metaanalysis was based on 1,728 effect sizes drawn from 151 unique samples from 96 studies of out-of-school adventure programs around the world. The study involved 12,057 participants of whom 72% were male and 28% female, ranging in age from 11 to 42 years.

Trusting oneself and others is a crucial learning of adventure programs.

Overall, the researchers found students made gains on 40 different individual outcomes which they categorized into six major categories: leadership (conscientiousness, decision making, general, teamwork, organizational ability, time management, values, and goals); self-concept (physical ability, peer relations, general self, physical appearance, academic, confidence, self-efficacy, family, self-understanding); academics (mathematics, reading, GPA, problem solving); personality (femininity, masculinity, achievement motivation, emotional stability, aggression, assertiveness, locus of control, maturity, neurosis reduction); interpersonal (cooperation, interpersonal communication, social competence, behavior, relating skills, recidivism); and adventure orientation (challengeness, flexibility, physical fitness, environmental awareness).

A theme underlying the outcomes with the greatest effects related to self-control (in the category of self-concept) and included independence, confidence, self-efficacy, self-understanding, assertiveness, internal locus of control, and decision-making—all critical resiliency traits. The researchers state, "Adventure programs appear to be most effective at providing participants with a sense of self-regulation" (p. 70).

A key finding of this study is that the students' gains INCREASED over time—sometimes months after participants completed the 20- to 26-day programs. This contrasts sharply to most educational—and certainly most prevention—

interventions in which program effects fade after the program terminates. "A program effect of .34 and a follow-up of an additional .17, leading to a combined pre-follow-up effect of .51, are unique in the education literature" (p. 70).

The researchers offer four premises about why adventure programs have these positive effects: 1) the intensity of the immediate experience, which allows the participant full involvement in the activity; 2) challenging and specific goals that direct attention and effort; 3) the amount and quality of feedback that is vital to the experiential learning process ("Feedback is the most powerful single moderator that improves affective and achievement outcomes."); and 4) mutual group support in which to reflect, dialogue, and act as well as to cope with and understand one's world (p. 75).From a resiliency/youth development perspective these positive findings are not difficult to explain. When young people's developmental needs for safety, belonging, challenge, respect, autonomy, mastery, and even meaning are met through caring relationships, challenging and high expectation messages and experiences, and opportunities for intense participation and contribution, healthy development unfolds—and keeps unfolding over time.

The researchers warn, however, that "Adventure programs are not inherently good. There is a great deal of variability in outcomes between different studies, different programs, and different individuals" (p. 77). According to the researchers, to the extent that a program incorporates the above principles, it is likely to be effective. This also illustrates that resiliency and youth development are not programs per se. It is *effective* adventure programs—just like *effective* preschool or mentoring programs—that produce these outstanding outcomes. As evaluation research has also shown, some adventure programs, like some preschool and mentoring programs, do not produce positive outcomes. The critical issue is not the program but the relationships and opportunities for participation that exist in the program. This speaks to the fact that it is HOW programs are done that is the key— what kind of role models exist and what environmental climate is created in programs, families, schools, and communities.

Students in the adventure learning program in Hardwick, VT, develop self-confidence by overcoming physical challenges with the help of their peers.

As I write this summary, the U.S. House of Representatives has just slipped by—mainly unnoticed by a media and public fixated on the private life of the president—a bill that would give states financial incentives for incarcerating 14- and 15- year-olds in adult prisons. From a political and policy perspective, all adults must ask themselves, their neighbors, their policymakers, why, WHY are we so willing to spend millions, even billions of dollars, locking up young people for longer and longer periods of time (more time than adults get for committing the same—usually nonviolent, drug-related—crime)?

There is ample research, this metaanalysis adding to the body of evidence, demonstrating the life-changing power of youth programs, even for gang-involved or troubled youth, that connect them to positive people, places, ideas, and interests that give their lives meaning and hope. In the words of drug policy researcher,

Physical risk-taking in an environment of safety is one component of adventure learning.

Elliott Currie (1993), "We have tried moral exhortation. We have tried neglect. We have tried punishment. We have even, more grudgingly, tried treatment. We have tried everything but improving lives" (p. 332). The research on resiliency and youth development programs shows precisely what this improvement looks like. It provides ammunition to fight for giving children and young people basic developmental supports and opportunities—with the people that care, the high expectations messages that challenge, and the places that welcome the voices and gifts of youth—that ultimately turn risk into resilience. ☀

References

Currie, E. (1993). *Reckoning: Drugs, the cities, and the American future*. New York: Hill and Wang.
Hattie, J., Marsh, H., Neill, J., & Richards, G. (1997). Adventure education and Outward Bound: Out-of-class experiences that make a lasting difference. *Review of Educational Research* 67(1), Spring, 43-87.

Bonnie Benard, M.S.W., has authored numerous articles and papers on resiliency and provides speeches and training on resiliency throughout the country. She can be reached at Resiliency Associates, 1238 Josephine, Berkeley, CA 94703, (p/f 510-528-4344), or by e-mail: bbenard@flash.net.

PART THREE

Additional Schoolwide and Classroom Strategies

Integrating Resiliency Building and Educational Reform: Why Doing One Accomplishes the Other

by Nan Henderson, M.S.W.

"We just don't have time to do *one more thing!*" Those of us who have worked in prevention over the past two decades are used to hearing this lament from well-intentioned, caring, but overwhelmed classroom teachers as they are confronted with the prospect of implementing another program. Though they agree that students need prevention programming, in their frustration they often express the feeling: Why does this, too, have to be *our* job?

Several years ago, when I started a new job as a prevention program administrator with Albuquerque Public Schools (APS), I had an experience that helped me realize that the cutting edge of prevention—strategies for building resiliency in students—is not simply *one more thing* for schools to do.

Another person joined the APS prevention team when I did. She didn't have a background in prevention, per se, but had excellent training and practice in facilitating school reform—called restructuring in our district at that time—in

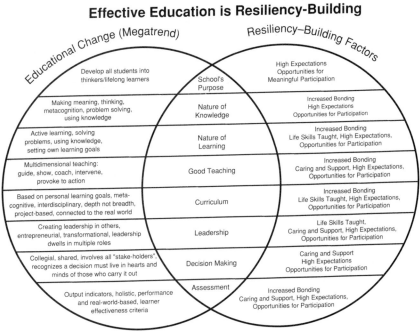

Effective Education is Resiliency-Building

Educational Change (Megatrend) — Resiliency–Building Factors

	School's Purpose	
Develop all students into thinkers/lifelong learners	School's Purpose	High Expectations, Opportunities for Meaningful Participation
Making meaning, thinking, metacognition, problem solving, using knowledge	Nature of Knowledge	Increased Bonding, High Expectations, Opportunities for Participation
Active learning, solving problems, using knowledge, setting own learning goals	Nature of Learning	Increased Bonding, Life Skills Taught, High Expectations, Opportunities for Participation
Multidimensional teaching: guide, show, coach, intervene, provoke to action	Good Teaching	Increased Bonding, Caring and Support, High Expectations, Opportunities for Participation
Based on personal learning goals, metacognitive, interdisciplinary, depth not breadth, project-based, connected to the real world	Curriculum	Increased Bonding, Life Skills Taught, High Expectations, Opportunities for Participation
Creating leadership in others, entrepreneurial, transformational, leadership dwells in multiple roles	Leadership	Life Skills Taught, Caring and Support, High Expectations, Opportunities for Participation
Collegial, shared, involves all "stake-holders", recognizes a decision must live in hearts and minds of those who carry it out	Decision Making	Caring and Support, High Expectations, Opportunities for Participation
Output indicators, holistic, performance and real-world-based, learner effectiveness criteria	Assessment	Increased Bonding, Caring and Support, High Expectations, Opportunities for Participation

from the book, *Resiliency in Schools: Making It Happen for Students and Educators* by Nan Henderson and Mike Milstein, published by Corwin Press, Thousand Oaks, CA, 1996.

dozens of schools throughout the district. When we began talking about our respective backgrounds, I eagerly shared with her the emerging prevention paradigm of resiliency which was just making a splash in 1991. My new colleague listened carefully as I talked about the key concepts. Then she said, "I've never heard of this resiliency stuff, but I can tell you that everything you are talking about is the basis of school restructuring."

A wonderful collaboration was born. Together we reached the conclusion which many others familiar with the fields of prevention and school reform have also realized: Effective school restructuring produces a resiliency-building school. And resiliency building in schools is actually the foundation of effective education.

Deborah Meier, principal of Central Park East in East Harlem, New York, where 90 % of the students graduate and 90 % of those go on to college (in a school district where the average graduation rate is 50 %) wrote in the July, 1995 issue of the *American School Board Journal* about her school's success: "There's a quality called 'hopefulness' that is a better predictor of success, even in college, than grade point average, class rank, or SAT score!" (p. 177). Reading about her school, it is clear that the all-important attitude of hope and optimism whatever the challenge, which I like to call "The Resiliency Attitude," permeates Central Park East. In addition, Meier reports her school integrates the trends in education documented in the diagram on page 55. Report after report of schools that are successful beyond the norm, including the schools that have been mentioned by the students interviewed for the "Faces of Resiliency" chapters in this book, characterize these schools similarly: Exceptional schools are imbued with that all-important attitude and are structured around resiliency principles—whether those involved realize it or not.

Helping educators understand this connection often brings a great relief and, in my experience, increased motivation to make the changes in their school that will *both* increase student academic success and foster greater life success in the form of less involvement in risky behaviors and increased resiliency. Helping preventionists realize this connection enables them to achieve what has been for us an historically elusive goal: Weaving the recommendations from prevention into the very fabric of schools. ❊

Nan Henderson, M.S.W., is a national speaker and consultant on fostering resiliency and wellness, alcohol and other drug issues, and on organizational change. She has co-authored/edited five books about resiliency, and is the Editor-in-chief at Resiliency In Action, Inc. She can be reached at Nan Henderson and Associates, 5130 La Jolla Blvd., #2K, San Diego, CA 92109, p/f (858-488-5034), or by e-mail: (nanh@connectnet.com).

Why Children Need Stories: Storytelling and Resiliency

by Linda Fredericks, M.A.

"Storytelling is an act of love. Sharing stories connects us to each other. When I tell my story, it connects to your story."—Njoki McElroy, teacher and storyteller (Young, 1993, p.21)

"The telling of stories is woven deep into the fabric of our lives...to know a story deeply and profoundly is to have a sense of belonging."—Michael E. Williams, author and storyteller (Williams, 1990, p.18)

"Story is the natural and intuitive medium of thought. It is the way our minds work."
—Vivian Gussin Paley, teacher and author (Paley, 1992, p.2)

A former colleague of mine, Dr. Mary Davis (1990), once related a moving experience that had happened to her several years before. She had been invited to an Indian reservation to give a talk on health promotion. She came dutifully armed with flip charts and overheads, and gave a carefully-structured presentation that included recent health statistics, research findings, and practical observations. At the conclusion of her talk she invited questions and comments from the audience. Several people raised their hands and asked questions about certain information she had shared or specific strategies that they could use.

> **"All the things you say have long been in our stories. We must simply love our children and tell them the stories again."**

After several moments, an older man who had sat in the back of the room slowly rose to his feet and looked at her steadily. In a quiet voice, he said, "All the things you say have long been in our stories. We must simply love our children and tell them the stories again." He then sat down and everyone in the room nodded their heads in silent agreement.

We must simply love our children and tell them the stories again. Those simple but poignant words have come to my mind often as I think about the power of storytelling. Stories are, after all, the most ancient, most compelling, and most intuitive form of communication, and are the means by which values and culture have been transmitted from generation to generation since the beginning of humankind. Whether the stories come from Hans Christian Anderson, an African griot, a Native American elder, or a Hispanic contadora, they all contain the secrets of living life with honesty, compassion, courage, and love. Stories help to bind people together, forge family and group identities, and create a sense of common culture and understanding. Any group—whether it be a family, a classroom, a workplace, or a civic organization—is defined by the stories that are known and shared between members.

Parents and other family members are usually the first, and often the most important storytellers that children know. Stories that are shared by parents or grandparents are often stories that are remembered for a lifetime, and provide endless guidance and inspiration to the child. When I conduct storytelling workshops for educators and other adults, I am always impressed by the vividness of memory and emotion that people have around the stories that they were told as small children. Participants often say things like, "I'll never forget that story my father used to read me at bedtime," or "I'll love reading stories to my own child because of how important it was to me when my grandmother would sit down after a meal and read a story to me."

> *"When family members tell stories to children, they are providing far more than just entertainment: They are supporting the healthy development of their children and conveying the most profound of life's lessons."*

When family members tell stories to children, they are providing far more than just entertainment: They are supporting the healthy development of their children and conveying the most profound of life's lessons. Through stories, children see that they are not alone in facing difficult and complex life issues. Through stories, they understand that there are other more productive ways of thinking, feeling, and acting that allow them to face actual situations with greater strength and wisdom. Stories provide a nonjudgmental means through which young people can safely examine ideas and feelings. Traditional stories from virtually every culture teach young people about the qualities that shape relationships and sustain all healthy human interactions. As Rives Collins and Pamela Cooper (1997) write in their book *The Power of Story*, "Stories help us make sense of our own experiences and understand the experiences of others" (p. 17).

Stories are also effective in increasing tolerance and understanding of people from other cultures. Through the medium of story, the listener can safely explore what all human beings have in common as well as how they differ from each other. Stories have the power to gently remove the child from his or her usual reality and for a time immerse the listener in a different time and place. As Ed Brody and Michael Punzak (1992) say in their introduction to the book *Spinning Tales, Weaving Hope: Stories of Peace, Justice and the Environment*, a well-told tale can take your mind and heart to places they have never been, let you experience events and emotions far from your daily routine, tailor itself to your own moods and reactions, and leave you with new dreams and insights" (p. 3). No one could return from an imaginative journey to another culture without retaining a greater appreciation for the unique wisdom and experiences of its people.

In addition to increasing tolerance and helping children grow emotionally and socially, there is also evidence that the process of storytelling can help enhance basic academic skills. Once they have heard or read a story, children of all ages are usually anxious to discuss what they have learned, so storytelling can be used by a parent or teacher to help children develop critical thinking skills. Storytelling can promote writing skills by encouraging young people to write their own stories, impressions of stories that they have heard, or even a play based upon a familiar tale. Children who hear stories will often improve their reading skills because they are interested in reading other related stories and information. Rives Collins, an associate professor of theater at Northwestern University and a storyteller who frequently performs at local schools, describes how children usually crowd the school library once he advises them—in low, conspiratorial tones—that the library is the source of the stories that he's just told them.

Research and writings in the areas of resiliency and human development shed further light on why stories are so important and irreplaceable in the lives of children.

Strengthening "Self-Righting Tendencies"

In their pioneering research on resiliency, Emmy Werner and Ruth Smith (1992) identified "self-righting tendencies" that move children toward normal adult development "under all but the most persistent adverse circumstances (p. 202)." When Werner and Smith conducted their longitudinal study of children who were at highest risk for developmental problems—children whose parents lived in poverty, abused substances, suffered from mental illness, and/or were physically violent—they were able to identify four basic internal characteristics possessed by resilient children: a sense of purpose and future, problem-solving skills, autonomy, and social competence. They found that one of the most important protective factors was an ongoing relationship with at least one person who provided the child with a secure basis for developing trust, caring, and initiative.

It is exactly these qualities that are key to the storytelling process. Stories that are passed from generation to generation teach young people that they have a bright future, that they are not alone, and that each individual has a special and unique purpose in life. At the same time, stories inevitably deal with conflict and reveal the necessity of persistence in the face of obstacles and hardships. Familiar fairy tales such as *Cinderella* or *The Ugly Duckling* not only portray the main characters facing a series of difficult trials, but show that the willingness to go through adversity is what allows the characters to become mature beings and triumph in life and in love.

In fact, dealing with life's challenges is not just incidental to traditional stories, but at their very heart. As Bruno Bettelheim (1989) emphasized in his classic book *The Uses of Enchantment*,

> *"Stories that are passed from generation to generation teach young people that they have a bright future, that they are not alone, and that each individual has a special and unique purpose in life."*

The message that fairy tales get across to the child in manifold form [is] that a struggle against severe difficulties in life is unavoidable, is an intrinsic part of human existence—but if one does not shy away, but steadfastly meets unexpected and often unjust hardships, one masters all obstacles and emerges victorious. (p. 8)

The great stories from throughout the world teach listeners that there is hope even in the darkest of circumstances, and that every person has reserves of possibilities and potential. In the words of authors Christina Feldman and Jack Kornfield (1991), "The stories of others serve as examples and guides for us, teaching us that the possibility of great courage, love, and compassion can be part of our own story" (p. 7).

Time-honored stories from virtually all cultures teach young people how to make decisions by discerning between good and evil, false and genuine, outer appearance and inner truth. In stories, as in life, all decisions have consequences, and the tales often contrast the aftermath of wise decisions with decisions that are foolish, uninformed, or downright malicious. The stories seem to challenge each listener by saying: "Look what happened to this person after she made this decision. What would you have done under similar circumstances?"

Stories promote social competence by showing the young person which qualities cause relationships to thrive, and which actions will sow distrust and discord. Stories convey the importance of truth and honesty in relationships, and emphasize the role of respect and caring between friends, family members, nations, young and old, teachers and students, humans and their environment.

At the same time that stories promote the crucial importance of relationships, they also teach young people the need to go out on their own and discover their identity. It is no accident that so many of the most beloved children's tales, such as *Hansel and Gretel* and *The Little Mermaid*, have to do with leaving home and making one's way in the world. All children are faced with issues of autonomy, and the stories guide them in understanding that the creation of a unique identity is a normal and healthy human need. As Bettelheim (1989) commented,

[Young people] intuitively comprehend that although these stories may be unreal, they are not untrue; that while what these stories tell about does not happen in fact, it must happen as inner experience and personal development; that [these] tales depict in imagery and symbolic form the essential steps in growing up and achieving a healthy and independent existence. (p. 73).

Storytelling itself can be a protective factor—not only because the content of the stories supports the resilient characteristics of children, but because the very act of storytelling fosters a caring and supportive relationship between an adult and young people. All manner of stories—fairy tales, folk tales, personal stories, etc.— help listeners to explore sensitive issues in a safe and nonthreatening way, provide appropriate models for behavior, and remind young people that they are not alone in their struggles and their pain.

Brain Development and Imagination

Storyteller Jay O'Callahan calls the process of storytelling "theater of the mind." When people listen to stories, they respond by creating vivid images of the characters and places and sounds and smells described by the words. This process of developing internal images and meaning in response to words is the basis of imagination.

While people of all ages benefit from frequent exposure to the imaginative process, its role in child development appears to be especially crucial. Author and educator Joseph Chilton Pearce (1992), in his provocative book *Evolution's End*, asserts that the repeated exposure to stories and the subsequent triggering of mental images stimulates appropriate neural development in the brain. It is the reason that children will insist on hearing the same story again and again—the hearing of a story causes neural pathways to form and strengthen within the brain, and the strengthened connections between the different parts of the brain allow the child to more easily incorporate additional learning. It is no wonder that Pearce quotes Albert Einstein as saying, "If you want your children to be brilliant, tell them fairy tales. If you want your children to be very brilliant, tell them even more fairy tales" (p. 154).

> *"The repeated exposure to stories and the subsequent triggering of mental images stimulates appropriate neural development in the brain. It is the reason that children will insist on hearing the same story again and again—the hearing of a story causes neural pathways to form and strengthen within the brain."*

Stories do not just help children develop a repertoire of mental images, but allow them to master the relationships between symbols, such as sorcerers, animals, or heroes, and the values that they stand for. The language of stories is metaphor—a symbol that represents something else. For example, in the well-known story of *Beauty and the Beast*, the Beast is a metaphor for someone who is basically good-natured, but who suffers from selfishness and arrogance. Beauty is a metaphor for a person who is kind and caring, but who has difficulty seeing beyond the surface to the inner beauty of another. The use of metaphor helps children to understand the true nature of the story characters and to take the lessons of the story—in this instance, seeing what people are like on the inside, not just on the outside; treating other people with kindness and respect—and apply them to their own lives.

It is not surprising, then, that researchers who study brain and behavioral development have identified imagination, not only as the essence of creativity, but as the basis for all higher order thinking. With imagination, with the ability to understand symbols, create solutions, and find meaning in ideas, young people are more capable of mastering language, writing, mathematics, and other learnings that are grounded in the use of symbols. Pearce (1992) claims that the repeated process of hearing time-honored children's tales and developing corresponding mental images is "the foundation... of everything we consider higher mentation or education" (p. 155).

While television provides stories, it also provides the images so that the brain is left unstimulated. Pearce suggests that while the content of television programs can be problematic, the greatest damage caused by frequent viewing is neural. This occurs because at precisely the time in a child's developmental process when brain development requires the creation of internal images, the television set is flooding the brain with external images. In other words, children who are exposed to massive quantities of television viewing will have greater difficulty developing a flow of images in response to verbal stimulus, and will subsequently have less opportunity for normal brain development. With the average child in the United States seeing 6,000 hours of television by his or her fifth year, there is legitimate concern that many children literally lack the brain development that will allow them to incorporate the abstract systems of alphabets and numbers.

> *"If you want your children to be brilliant, tell them fairy tales. If you want your children to be very brilliant, tell them even more fairy tales."*
> —Albert Einstein

The capacity for imagination has profound implications, not just for academic learning, but for behavior as well. Several recent studies have shown that children who lack imagination are not only prone to school failure, but are far more susceptible to violence. Such children cannot imagine alternatives to their immediate perceptions of anger or hostility; they are able to react only to what they believe is the situation in front of them. In the words of researcher Ronald Slaby (1994) at the Education Development Center at Harvard University, aggressive young people are more likely "to define their problems in hostile ways, adopt oppositional goals, seek fewer facts, have less insight into alternative solutions, and fail to anticipate the negative consequences of their behavior" (p. 1).

The correlation between lack of imagination and violence makes perfect sense, since unimaginative children will encounter continual frustration and failure in their academic pursuits as well as their relationships with others. What healthy human relationship can exist without creativity and imagination? On the other hand, children who possess imagination have a very different experience. They can be exposed to the same hostile situation as an aggressive child, but rather than causing the situation to escalate into greater hostility, they have the ability to imagine, and therefore act upon, different solutions. They can create images in their mind that are different than what is apparent in their present surroundings. They are cognizant of the impact of their actions, and can see the link between their present behavior and future events.

The Importance of Both Storytelling Content and Process

As Pearce has shown, it is both the content and the process of storytelling that is important for the cultivation of imagination and intelligence. The content of stories helps young people to learn about the value that all life possesses, provides them with valuable role models, and teaches them strategies to cope with a variety of life situations. The process of storytelling fosters brain development in young children, helps them develop the capacity for metaphorical/symbolic thought which underlies all academic and social learning, and endows them with imagination.

By sharing stories with their children and discussing the lessons embedded in the stories, parents, other family members, and other caring adults can help young people find the parallels between the stories and their

> *"Children who are exposed to massive quantities of television viewing will have greater difficulty developing a flow of images in response to verbal stimulus, and will subsequently have less opportunity for normal brain development."*

own experiences. The stories help young people to understand that there are helpful and productive ways to approach the difficult issues of their own lives, and give them the tools to make positive changes. Adults can make a large difference in the lives of children by taking the time to "tell the stories again."

References

Bettelheim, B. (1989). *The uses of enchantment: The meaning and importance of fairy tales.* New York: Random House.

Brody, B., Goldspinner, J., et al. (1992). *Spinning tales, weaving hope: Stories of peace, justice, and the environment.* Philadelphia, PA: New Society Publishers.

Collins, R., & Cooper, P. (1997). *The power of story: Teaching through storytelling.* Scottsdale, AZ: Gorsuch Scarisbrick.

Davis, M. (1990). Tell the stories again—arts as prevention. *Prevention Perspectives,* March/April. Boulder, CO: Prevention Center.

Feldman, C., & Kornfield, J. (1991). *Stories of the spirit, stories of the heart: Parables of the spiritual path from around the world.* New York: Harper Collins.

Fredericks, L. (1996). *Prevention through storytelling.* Oak Brook, IL: North Central Regional Educational Laboratory.

Paley, V.G. (1992). In the beginning there was storytelling. *Humanities, (3)* 1.

Pearce, J.C. (1992). *Evolution's end: Claiming the potential of our inheritance.* New York: Harper Collins.

Slaby, R. (1994). Quoted in *The Safe and Drug Free School Newsletter,* Fall. La Jolla, CA: Family and Relationship Center.

Werner, E., & Smith, R. (1992). *Overcoming the odds: High risk children from birth to adulthood.* Ithaca, NY: Cornell University Press.

Williams, M.E. (1990). Voices from unseen rooms: storytelling and community. *Weavings, A Journal of Christian Spiritual Life, (5)* 5.

Young, C.T. (1993). The storyteller. *Northwest Perspective, (6)* 4.

Linda Fredericks, M.A. is an educational consultant specializing in evaluation, publications development, and resiliency-based training programs. She is also an experienced storyteller who has lectured extensively on the link between storytelling and healthy human development, and recently authored a manual on storytelling for the North Central Regional Educational Laboratory (NCREL). She can be reached by phone or e-mail (303-545-6051; lindaf@indra.com).

Youth Communication: A Model Program for Fostering Resilience Through the Art of Writing

by Al Desetta, M.A., and Sybil Wolin, Ph.D.

Lives are stories, and each person's stories hold the potential for many tellings. Every telling is an interpretation. Authors can draw themselves as they choose. From multitudes of events, they can select the incidents that impress them most to construct a plot that recounts defeats, successes, and possibilities. In turn, the story they tell exerts a powerful influence on their feelings and behavior. As they construct their story, it constructs them (Wolin & Wolin, 1993).

The narrative school of psychotherapy capitalizes on the inherent subjectivity in life stories to foster the process of repairing psychological harm. A principle technique of this school is *reframing*, opening up hidden themes that have been frozen shut in memory. This theory of therapeutic change holds that by recognizing previously unseen elements of their struggles, clients will reinterpret themselves—construct a new life story that will be the basis for living well in the present and regarding the future with greater optimism.

According to a study done at Project Resilience in Washington, D.C., the art of reframing and the psychological growth that results is not the therapist's provenance alone. Writers have known its power all along, and so do many youth who struggle ceaselessly and actively to overcome lives burdened by terrible adversity.

> "The art of reframing and the psychological growth that results is not the therapist's provenance alone. Writers have known its power all along."

The Project Resilience study was based on interviews with 25 adults who had grown up knowing some combination of poverty, neglect, abuse, racism, violence, addictions, and family dysfunction. All 25 had bruises that attested to their experiences. But they were also remarkably resilient, breaking out of the cycle of troubles in which they began their lives. In answer to the question, "How did you do it?", many recounted how they relied on writing to gain insight into their lives and how that insight, in turn, was central to repairing the harm they had suffered.

Youth Communication: Fostering Resilience through Writing

The process of repairing by writing described by many of the participants in the Project Resilience study is being actively taught and promoted at Youth Communication in New York City. A non-profit youth development organization, it publishes two magazines written by teens for teens, *Foster Care Youth United* and *New Youth Connections*. The program is a model of how courage and hope can be fostered in youth who struggle daily to prevail.

By teaching the craft of writing personal essays and by publishing their work in two magazines, Youth Communication offers young people the opportunity to discover, affirm, strengthen, and expand their resilience. In turn, thousands of teens who read the magazines are encouraged by their example.

Youth Communication's stated mission is to use writing to help teens "reflect on their lives and acquire the skills and information they need to make thoughtful choices." Although fostering resilience and producing therapeutic effects are not explicitly stated goals of the organization, both are implicit in its

> *"The heart of the program is the extended process of engaging youth in revising drafts of their stories repeatedly, sometimes six or seven times. Revising in this context is the equivalent of reframing in the therapist's office."*

mission. The heart of the program is the extended process of engaging youth in revising drafts of their stories repeatedly, sometimes six or seven times. Revising in this context is the equivalent of reframing in the therapist's office.

Working one-on-one with adult editors, the young writers at Youth Communication aim for publishable stories. In order to do so, they must master the basics of spelling, grammar, and punctuation. They must also learn to accept criticism, engage in explorations of truthfulness and fairness, and accept responsibility for doing their work, for its final quality, and for the effect it will have on its readers. The editor-writer relationship at Youth Communication goes beyond the mechanics of writing to the deeper purpose of reconstructing and re-envisioning the self's experience and relationship with others. The stories that have emerged from Youth Communication, while often laden with pain, also reflect the remarkable resilience it took not only to live them but also to commit them to writing.

A close look at how one Youth Communication writer crafted her story reveals the learning, self awareness, and personal growth that occur when a young writer speaks to an audience of peers.

Wunika Hicks: Facing the Problem

Wunika Hicks was one of the very first writers to join the magazine *Foster Care Youth United*, and she worked on the staff for five years. When she joined the magazine, she was 16 and had been living in foster care for eight years.

In an essay she wrote as part of her application to join the program, Wunika

> *"The stories that have emerged from Youth Communication, while often laden with pain, also reflect the remarkable resilience it took not only to live them but also to commit them to writing."*

spoke about her anger at having been separated for several years from David, her only sibling, who had been adopted out of foster care while she remained in the system. "How can they take the only real blood that you have away from you?" Wunika plaintively asked.

She chose to write on this topic for her first article. Her first very brief and handwritten draft began with the scene of her hearing the news that David was going to be adopted. She went on to describe her despair over the separation, her unsuccessful attempts to see him (it was a closed adoption), and her frustrations with social workers who came and went but never helped her locate her brother. Wunika ended her first draft on what seemed to be a false note: a "Kool-Aid" smile and an appreciation for her foster mother's promise to help her locate David. In actuality, her foster mother had virtually no chance of finding Wunika's brother, and Wunika knew it. Nevertheless, she stated:

> My [foster] mother came to me and said, "Wunika, I going to get a lawyer to look into this further."
>
> Even though I had tears running down my cheeks, I put on a big Kool-Aid smile. It showed me how much she cares for me. I'm glad I've come in this house because she understands me!
>
> How many foster mothers can you say that about?

> *"Set aside what you know and take a fresh look. What's at the heart of this? What's important that you haven't yet said? Look at it whole and find an image, a word, a phrase to capture your difficulty [in moving ahead]."*

In addition to the compromised integrity of her ending, Wunika began her story without the background context needed to understand her family's history. Enter her editor, who began the necessary revising process by pointing out the flaws in the story. In the therapist's lexicon, the story revealed "denial," a psychological symptom of dysfunction. It was ripe for reframing. In the editor's vocabulary, it was unauthentic and incomplete; it would not convince a reader. The difference is more than semantic. It introduces a third party, the reading audience, whose presence can diffuse the tension of confrontation that can develop in the therapeutic dialogue and is often the major stumbling block in treating teens. No longer does the teen need to "own" his or her denial to get better, to please the therapist, to conform to the therapeutic contract. Now the point is to write a story that others will want to read and believe.

To set the process of revision in motion, the editor used an exercise called "Guidelines for Composing" that aims, like reframing, to get below the surface of the story and uncover hidden themes. The exercise begins concretely enough by posing questions about the content. In this case, the editor asked how Wunika felt about David's adoption. He then zeroed in on the stuck quality of her writing by asking these questions: "Set aside what you know and take a fresh look. What's at the heart of this? What's important that you haven't yet said? Look at it whole and find an image, a word, a phrase to capture your difficulty [in moving ahead]."

In response to the exercise and out of motivation to tell her story well by honing her writing, Wunika's denial began to lift, and her insight began to blossom.

In response to her editor's questions, she wrote the following:

> I guess I feel it was my fault that he's being adopted. Being I was eight years old and stuck in the house to watch him, I hated him for a while. I feel it is coming back to me now because I don't have him at all, and I want him.

Writing as a Vehicle to Personal Honesty

Clearly, the Guidelines exercise enabled Wunika to gather her strength and give voice to something that had not been expressed in her first draft nor in her conversations with her editor: her guilt that her brother's adoption was somehow her fault. It also revealed a crucial detail. Wunika had to care for her brother before he was adopted (she was "stuck in the house" with him because of this). The recognition of her burden opened up the emotional core of the story, and in essence, provided the basic three-part structure it would assume during revision: 1) I was mother to my brother; 2) I resented him for it; 3) He was adopted, and now I feel angry and guilty.

Through several more revisions, Wunika's insight and ability to be honest with herself grew as she added previously omitted background material to her story. She wrote about how her mother, who had been left to raise both of her children after her husband's death, would be gone for days at a time, leaving Wunika home alone to care for David. She developed, in greater detail, her complicated emotions toward her brother when they went together into foster care—how she rejected him once she was relieved of the burden of being his "mother." She was able to express her previously suppressed feelings of guilt that her actions had caused David's adoption.

> *"Through several more revisions, Wunika's insight and ability to be honest with herself grew as she added previously omitted background material to her story."*

The end of her final draft, completed after many weeks, reflected her personal progress. No longer was it a tribute to her foster mother, made with a false "Kool-Aid smile." Rather it was transformed into an honest and fully articulated description of her difficult emotions related not only to being separated from her mother and father but also from the only family remaining to her while she had been in foster care.

"I Lost My Brother to Adoption" (published in 1993 and reprinted here on p. 69 with permission from Youth Communication), Wunika's first published story in *Foster Care Youth United,* was followed over the years by a series of interrelated essays in which she explored her complex feelings about her biological mother, her foster mother, and her long years in foster care.

Wunika's stories can be found in *The Heart Knows Something Different: Teenage Voices from the Foster Care System* (Persea Books, 1996), a recently published volume of the best stories selected from *Foster Care Youth United.* In each of these essays, her brother and his loss to adoption are constants, sometimes

> *"The process of writing and revising in which Wunika was acheived and the results she acheived can be generalized to other aspects of her life and become a source of the strength and hope she will need to overcome the stumbling blocks life has strewn in her path."*

mentioned briefly, sometimes viewed from a new angle, but always there. The entire body of her work, though laced with pain, shines with her resilience—her courage and her persistence—to break through her denied feelings and speak the truth.

Generalizing the Process of Writing to Other Parts of One's Life

Our belief is that the process of writing and revising in which Wunika was engaged and the results she acheived can be generalized to other aspects of her life and become a source of the strength and hope she will need to overcome the stumbling blocks life has strewn in her path. It is a considered belief based on the the knowledge of what has happpned to large numbers of youth who have participated in Youth Communication. Years later, many report that working there was a turning point in their lives that helped them gain confidence and skills required in their subsequent education and careers. Some have overcome tremendous obstacles to become journalists, writers, and novelists. Hundreds more are working in law, teaching, business, and other careers. Undoubtedly, their success has been determined by many factors, but among them the personal growth achieved through writing for an audience of readers cannot be overestimated.

References

Wolin, S.J., & Wolin S. (1993). *The resilient self: How survivors of troubled families rise above adversity.* New York: Villard Books.

Youth Communication (1996). *The heart knows something different: Teenage voices from the foster care system.* New York: Persea Books.

Sybil Wolin, Ph.D., is founder and co-director of Project Resilience, which offers training and consultation to clinicians, educators, and prevention specialists. She co-authored The Resilient Self: How Survivors of Troubled Families Rise Above Adversity *and is featured in the educational video* Survivor's Pride: Building Resilience in Youth at Risk *(Attainment Co., Inc., 1994). She has lectured on the topic of resilience across the United States and abroad and can be reached at Project Resilience in Washington, D.C. (202-966-8171).*

Al Desetta, M.A., is founding editor of Foster Care Youth United, *published by Youth Communication. He has also served as editor of New Youth Connections, the organization's general interest magazine for teenagers, as instructor in its juvenile prison writing project, and as director of its teacher development program. He is the editor of* The Heart Knows Something Different: Teenage Voices from the Foster Care System, *an anthology of personal narratives first published in* Foster Care Youth United. *He can be reached at Youth Communication in New York City (212-242-3270).*

I Lost My Brother to Adoption

by Wunika Hicks

When I was just eight years old, I became a mother to my brother. I had to stay home all day to take care of David, who wasn't even a year old. My mother was never home. She'd be out trying to find a job, to make some money so we could have a decent meal. My father had passed away when I was two.

So I had to do everything my mother couldn't do—make David's bottles, change his Pampers (yuk!), wash him, and rock him to sleep. I'm surprised I didn't get left back because I hardly went to school. Do you know how it feels to look out the window in the morning and see other kids with their book bags while you're stuck in the house?

I really began to dislike David. I felt that if he had never been born I wouldn't have this responsibility. I felt it was his fault that I was restricted from doing the things that every young child wants to do.

So it was a relief in a way when my brother and I were placed in a foster home. I was turning nine years old and my brother was fifteen months. We were taken away because of my mother's neglect.

I didn't want to be separated from my mother. She tried so hard to keep us together. But on the other hand I was happy that I could go to school on a regular basis and play in the park with children my own age, since my foster parents would now take care of David.

Still, I hated being around my brother. I wanted him out of my sight. I treated David so badly. He wanted me to play with him or take him to the store because I had been more of a mother to him than our real mother. But although he wanted my attention I ignored him or pushed him away, because all I could see was the past, those endless days when I was stuck with him in the house.

When my foster mother saw the way I treated David, she would say to me, "One day you're going to wish you had a brother." But I didn't pay her any mind.

Eventually I moved into a new foster home. I was thirteen. I was hurt when I left my old foster family because I had been with them for almost five years, but the new home turned out to be much better. They treated me like their own. In the meantime, David stayed with our old foster family.

It wasn't long before my social worker told me my brother, now age six, would be moving to a new foster home, too. But there was a twist: the social worker said that my brother's new foster parents wanted to adopt him.

When she told me this, I stood up and just walked around the room. I was in complete shock. My body was numb and I began to cry. Was this really going on? I suddenly felt so protective of David. I hadn't wanted the responsibility of being his mother, but now I didn't want anyone taking him away.

I felt it was my fault that he was being adopted. I felt the past was coming back to haunt me. I wanted David now, but when I had him I rejected him. All I could hear was my old foster mother saying, *"One day you're going to wish you had a brother."* I asked my social worker if I could still see David after he was adopted. She told me that his new parents would make that decision. She also told me that they wanted to change my brother's name—not only his last name, but his first name too. "How can they do this?" I asked the social worker. "What gives them that right? I took care of him. I'm more of a mother to him than anyone could ever be. I know what he likes and dislikes. I'm his mother, I'm his sister, I'm everything to him! I'm all the family he has—me, not some strangers!"

The social worker just looked at me. She could see the pain I was going through, but all she could say was, "That's the law." I asked my social worker to find out if they'd allow me to see David. She said a good time for a visit would be around Christmas vacation, if the adoptive parents agreed. I was happy that I'd finally get to see him.

But before the visit could be arranged, my social worker transferred to a different department. Later I found out that the adoptive parents never even answered my request for visitation rights.

A few months later I got a new social worker, but she didn't care that I missed my brother. All she did was sit there and smoke. Pretty soon, she left too.

(I can't help but think that if I hadn't been running from social worker to social worker, I might have been able to see my brother by now. I've been in foster care for eight years and I think I've had six social workers, five law guardians, and counting.)

The third social worker was better. At least she listened. I told her my problems, but she told me that when my brother was adopted, his records were sealed. That meant I couldn't find out where he lived, much less visit him.

I couldn't cry. The tears wouldn't come. I had cried so much that I didn't have any tears left. I felt completely alone and helpless. I had tried so hard but I hadn't gotten anywhere. I didn't have anyone who understood me.

I ran home. My foster mother asked me what was wrong, and I told her how they gave me the runaround. She got in touch with my law guardian, who is looking into this matter now.

I still feel my brother's adoption is my fault. I should have been there for David when he needed me and not pushed him away. I'm a blood relative, but I turned him away when he needed me most. I could have at least showed him I loved him. Now he's in a complete stranger's home. I haven't seen him for three years. I don't know where he lives. I don't even know his new name.

And I didn't have a chance to say goodbye. The last time I saw him—in the playroom at our agency—I didn't know it would be the last time. I walked past him without saying anything, thinking I'd see him again the next day.

One of the last things he said to me was, "I hate Wunika," because I had told my social worker I didn't want to see him anymore. That was when I was sick of him, just before he was going to be adopted.

I think of David every day—so much that it hurts. It hurts the most when his birthday passes. He's getting older without me.

I hope he hasn't forgotten me but remembers the times I took care of him as a mother. I don't want him to remember the times I rejected him.

I may have pushed him away when he wanted me, but that doesn't mean I don't love him. The system didn't understand my history, my pain. They took away the only family I had. Now I don't have anyone to love.

I just hope it all works out and that I do get to see my brother one day.

Wunika Hicks was 16 when she wrote, "I Lost My Brother to Adoption" and, soon after, "She'll Always Be My Mother." Born in Brooklyn, Wunika entered foster care at age eight and spent the next 10 years in the system, mostly with foster families. Writing about her experiences "opened up a lot of doors, because I had locked my feelings inside." In 1995, she enrolled as a freshman at the State University College at Brockport in upstate New York. She is also the author of two other essays in The Heart Knows Something Different, *"Sista on the Run (From the Past)" and "A Vacation from Mr. Hope."*

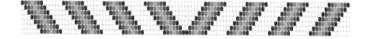

Caring Classroom Nurtures Children's Resilience

The following is reprinted from the March, 1995 Western Center News, *published by the now discontinued Western Regional Center for Drug-free Schools and Communities.*

by Andrew Duncan

"Meeting children's basic needs for caring and connectedness; for respect, challenge, and structure; and for meaningful involvement, belonging, and power should be the primary focus of any prevention, education, and treatment intervention with children," says Bonnie Benard. Benard has synthesized the research findings on resiliency and summarized them parsimoniously into the resilience traits of "social competence, problem solving, autonomy, and a sense of a bright future; and the environmental protective factors of caring and support, high expectations, and opportunities for participation."

In an effective school, the protective factors of caring and support are seen in the relationships established with and among children, teachers, and families; high expectations ensure success for all kids, foster high self-esteem in children, teachers, and families, and build on family strengths; and opportunities for participation get children, teachers, and families involved in decision making and planning, helping others, and engaging children and parents in the learning process.

Teachers of young children have long known that good, developmentally appropriate teaching contributes not only to academic growth, but also to mental and emotional well-being. At Stayton Elementary School in Oregon's Willamette Valley, teacher-of-the-year Kathy Cheval routinely incorporates into her teaching the protective factors that foster resiliency in kids.

Walking the Talk

The first thing you notice when you enter Cheval's second grade classroom is the layout. This is no traditional classroom. Groups of tables form work stations of varying boxes. A carpeted reading area includes a rocking chair, cushions, and a large couch resplendent with pillows and an enormous teddy bear. A computer center murmurs exotic beeps and assorted animal noises. Brightly colored boxes of learning materials sit invitingly on almost every square inch of shelf space.

Some 28 children and four adults share the space. The room is filled with a quiet, subdued buzz of activity. At one table, Cheval works with a reading group; at another, a teacher's aide helps children with a language assignment. In the reading center, some children sit on the carpet at a listening center, while others share big books. Three are curled up on the couch, engrossed in their books, and two others are reading aloud to a parent volunteer. Two students work cooperatively at the computer, animatedly discussing the problems they had chosen, and laughing as they succeed in solving them. Another volunteer sits in a corner surrounded by a group of children who want to practice the new vocabulary for the day.

A visitor to the room immediately becomes a part of the learning environment. "Would you help me with my language, please?" one boy asks. Announces another child, "This is David. He just came to our school. I'm helping him." It is in this snug, safe environment that one sees the protective factors in action.

Caring and Support

Hugs and smiles are shared in this classroom. A hug to welcome you to school, a quick "squeeze" for a job well done, a smile and nod of encouragement—all these are ways that adults and children alike show their caring. But it goes beyond that!

A sleepy, bleary-eyed boy wanders into the classroom late. A hug from Cheval is followed by her query: "John, did you have breakfast yet? No? Quickly go ask the cook of she'll give you breakfast." John returns 15 minutes later looking refreshed and awake, and is unobtrusively integrated into the classroom activities.

David, the new boy, is standing alone. "David," Cheval addresses him with a smile, "would you help Margaret clean up these materials? We need them before we start the lesson." David looks lost for a moment, then Margaret says. "See? You do it like this." Within moments, David is talking animatedly and is involved in his task.

The pervasive caring that is so evident in the classroom goes beyond its walls. Cheval has an extensive networking system set up to communicate her caring to parents. She actively enlists their help in the classroom, and keeps them busy with meaningful tasks when they are there. She sends home newsletters about the classroom

> *"The all-important relationships between children are fostered in this classroom by child-developed 'rights and responsibilities' which prohibit put-downs and affirm healthy social behavior."*

activities every week, and solicits feedback from parents. When there are problems or issues to be resolved, she (and often the child involved) phones to enlist the parents' help. She also makes it a point to phone at least one parent each week to report an achievement or improvement.

The all-important relationships between children are fostered in this classroom by child-developed "rights and responsibilities" which prohibit put-downs and affirm healthy social behavior. Problem-solving skills have been taught and practiced in role-play situations, and students are expected to use these strategies before seeking intervention from the teacher. Appropriate behaviors and problem-solving skills are modeled by the adults in the room, and are constantly affirmed and reinforced. As a result, children in the room treat one another with kindness and consideration, and readily volunteer to help one another. Outbursts and finger pointing are rare occurences.

Caring is also fostered by active involvement with younger children. Each week the children spend time with their "kindergarten buddies," reading to them and sharing their experiences. "I really love to read to my buddy," bubbles Rachel, "and she really likes it, too!"

"The benefits to kindergartners are self-evident," says Cheval, "but my second graders gain a lot too. They all get the opportunity to be leaders—I really emphasize the importance of being a good role model. They get to practice reading in an 'interesting and excited' way. Most importantly, being looked up to by a little person really helps develop their self-concept!"

High Expectations

High expectations for herself and for the class are the norm in Cheval's room. Social, behavioral, and work expectations are clear. The students developed the basic rules—student rights and responsibilities—under which the room operates. Everyone has the right to:

- Be safe (don't do things that might hurt yourself or others)
- Be treated with kindness (give compliments, not put-downs)
- Be heard (be a good listener)
- Learn (don't distract other people)

Behavioral and work expectations are delineated constantly in the classroom, hallways, and lunchroom. "When someone is speaking, you need voices off and eyes on the speaker," Cheval reminds the students. Other reminders might include these: "I expect your best quality work," or "We walk quietly in the hallway so that we don't interfere with other kids' learning."

> *"By spending time at the beginning of the year, I find that the kids learn to solve conflicts in appropriate ways. In the long run, I end up spending less time intervening."*

Appropriate behaviors are reinforced by quiet, usually private, praise. Inappropriate behaviors are dealt with by private conferences and opportunities to "try again." Rather than externally imposed discipline, problem solving is the key to conflict resolution:

- Identify the problem
- Identify the inappropriate course of action
- List options for next time
- Role-play as appropriate

"This is time consuming," Cheval says. "But by spending time at the beginning of the year, I find that the kids learn to solve conflicts in appropriate ways. In the long run, I end up spending less time intervening, and the kids develop some really important skills."

Incentives accentuate the positive. The class earns time that may be used for social activities. Sanctions emphasize logical consequences; for instance, throwing paper would result in a child spending time cleaning up the classroom.

Work expectations vary from child to child. All children are expected to do their best and are encouraged to do so, but Cheval helps where necessary. Some students receive personal assistance from a teacher or aide, some get time with parent volunteers.

Where special circumstances demand it, Cheval makes special provisions. One child, Billy, whose parent had a serious substance abuse problem, has few opportunities to work at home and is clearly reluctant to leave school each day. Cheval set up an after-school program involving helping the teacher prepare for the next day, a short period of intensive one-on-one reading instruction, followed by some independent time on the computer as a "reward." Interestingly, Billy's favorite computer game is a math skills program, one of his weaker subjects. In the two months since Billy started on his special after-school program, he has made dramatic advances in his academic work, spends more time on tasks in the regular classroom, and has reduced the level of his attention-seeking behavior. "He is a capable child," says Cheval. "All he needs is a chance to show what he *can* do."

Participation

Other key factors in fostering resiliency are that children are actively involved in planning and decision making, and that they are actively engaged in the learning process. In Cheval's room, both are evident. As already noted, the children in the class play a key role in establishing and monitoring students' rights and responsibilities, and in setting standards for academic and social behaviors.

The kids also are responsible for "running" the room—they set things up, clean up afterward, and inspect the clean-up. "They're tougher than I would be," Cheval says.

While all children are expected to complete certain assignments and activities, there is a great deal of individual choice about when tasks are done. For instance, aside from the direct instruction in reading and language arts, children have a variety of tasks to complete, including reading silently, reading aloud, listening, and writing. During reading center time, children decide which activity they wish to do. Some of the activities are required, while some are "free choice." Additionally, some activities are limited by, for instance, the availability of headsets at the listening center, or the availability of a parent volunteer to listen to reading. Children must plan their activities and work cooperatively with others to accomplish their goals. Their choices and planning are supported by "to do" checklists prepared by Cheval and by constant monitoring and encouragement by the adults in the room.

"One of the key factors in providing children with decision-making opportunities is to do so within a framework," explains Cheval, "If you present a child with a large plateful of different candies, and ask him to choose one, the decision will take a very long time, and even after he chooses, he won't be sure he made the best choice. If you present him with three or four candies, he will be able to choose right away and be satisfied with his choice. So it is in the classroom. Children can feel successful in making decisions when they are not overwhelmed by the possibilities."

At the beginning of the year, children are not given choices in activities. Within a week or two they are given two choices: "You can do this, or that." Within a few weeks as the children develop the ability to make choices, the range of choices is expanded, but supported with strategies to ensure the child's success.

Engagement in learning is fundamental to Cheval's teaching style. In her classroom one rarely sees teacher-centered "chalk and talk" whole group instruction. Nearly all teacher-directed instruction occurs in small groups focused on individual abilities and needs. Much of the rest of the learning occurs in cooperative groups or with partners. On occasion, children choose to work independently. This is not to suggest that this is a laissez-faire classroom; on the contrary, although learning occurs in a child-centered cooperative framework, careful preparation and high expectations set the scene for high levels of engagement and participatory learning.

> **"Nearly all teacher-directed instruction occurs in small groups focused on individual abilities and needs."**

Math is taught using some whole-group instruction, followed by skills practice. Those intriguing boxes mentioned earlier contain (among other things) an enormous variety of math skill-building activities. The children can choose to work in groups, in pairs, or independently. Science is taught almost exclusively using hands-on science experiments emphasizing the scientific method. Choice in writing tasks is provided during "writers workshop" activities.

Active participation is not limited to children in this classroom. Cheval actively solicits parent involvement and has many regular volunteers, "The key to using parent volunteers," says Cheval, "is to have them actively involved with the kids."

Cheval's room is one of many at Stayton Elementary School that exemplify the protective factors that foster resiliency. The school has had a site-based team for many years; child-centered, developmentally appropriate learning is emphasized; and professional development is ongoing. Principal Randy LaFollett has a "daily dozen" task list that includes only three administrative items. The rest are communication and support activities that foster resiliency in children, families, and staff.

References

Benard, Bonnie. (1994). *Applications of resilience: Possibilities and promise.* Paper presented at the Conference on the Role of Resilience in Drug Abuse, Alcohol Abuse, and Mental Illness. Washington D.C.

AUTHOR'S NOTE: Kathy Cheval has taught in California and Germany, been an instructor in the Elementary Education Program at Western Oregon State College, as well as teaching at Stayton Elementary School, where she was "Teacher of the Year" in 1994.

Tonya Benally: "School is the Only Family I Have"

by Nan Henderson, M.S.W.

"Most longitudinal studies of resilient children have noted that they enjoy school, whether nursery school, grade school, or high school and make it a 'home away from home,' a refuge from a dysfunctional household," wrote Emmy Werner in her Foreword to Resiliency in Schools: Making It Happen for Students and Educators, *published in 1996 by Corwin Press.*

"The more successful inner-city schools tend to maintain realistically high academic standards, provide effective feedback with ample praise, and offer positions of trust and responsibility to their students," she adds. *"Such structural support appears to be an especially potent protective factor for children from divorce-prone homes and minority backgrounds."*

Tonya Benally, profiled below, is a living example of Emmy Werner's words. Her story demonstrates the power of a school to be "like family," and to provide—in Tonya's case—self-respect, pride, and a vision of a positive future.

Tonya Benally says she used to take the problems she experienced at home "out on myself." She explained that she was in so much pain in a family where she felt a "lack of love and respect and support" she tried suicide three times as a way of dealing with her family problems. "Deep inside it hurt me so bad I couldn't take it anymore," she said, "because they blame me, they criticize me, and it was hard." Tonya's dad was physically abusive, drank a lot, and left when she was 13. But her family has yet to heal.

> **"'The only time I felt good about myself was when I went to school,' Tonya says of the two years of her life during which she attended an alternative school, Gallup Central, in Gallup, New Mexico."**

Tonya, however, has changed. Now in her 20s, she says, "Well that's their problem." And the biggest factor in Tonya's healing was school.

"The only time I felt good about myself was when I went to school," Tonya says of the two years of her life during which she attended an alternative school, Gallup Central, in Gallup, New Mexico. She described what happened to her there: "I [asked] the people at school, 'Why do you put up with me?' 'Because you're so good' [they answered]. I was like, 'Yeah, right.' You know I tried to put myself down in front of my teachers and they'd say, 'You're not like that, Tonya.' It just blew the negative thoughts out of my mind. And I felt good for the rest of the day."

> *"The teachers were paying more attention to you. I didn't usually get this attention. But the more they made it fun and exciting, the more I wanted to be there. [These things] encouraged me every day to go to school.... And I really put effort in."*

School was not always such a positive place for Tonya. She went to a traditional high school before attending Gallup Central, and by the time she was 15 she was failing. She was using alcohol and other drugs, partially as a way to try to cope with the pain of her family situation, and was "ditching school all the time, drinking on campus, and getting suspended." Then she heard about a new alternative school opening in Gallup and she decided to enroll.

"At first it felt kind of funny," Tonya said "because the teachers were paying more attention to you. I didn't usually get this attention. But the more they made it fun and exciting, the more I wanted to be there. [These things] encouraged me every day to go to school.... And I really put effort in."

Tonya had special praise for the school librarian, Ms. Hill. Tonya described her as "always nice, smiling, giving us compliments. When I go in there, a frown on my face, she says, 'What's wrong?' She just brightens your day, and you forget

> *"They told us, [that] we are a family. We heard that from the principal all the time. That's why I went to school every day."*

about all the bad things. At one point, I wasn't really doing my work. She used to tell me, 'Tonya, you go sit down over there and I won't let anybody bother you.' And she was real. She said, 'If it makes you feel better, I'll do my work, too.'" Tonya added, "She puts a different perspective on life for us, you know. The library felt like my home because she was always there."

Tonya liked the size of her school, only 150 students, and the fact that though the students are several ethnicities, including Native American, Hispanic, and Caucasian, they all get along. She also commented on all the different activities in the school, including a ropes course, numerous field trips, and parties and movies that the faculty plans.

"They told us, 'We are a family.' We heard that from the principal all the time. That's why I went to school every day. Because people there respected me and talked to me. I don't get that much attention at home. And there's a lot of things that I did not do in [traditional] high school that I wanted to do."

> *"Tonya still can't quite believe the way her life turned around. 'getting As and Bs and I used to have Ds and Fs all the time.'"*

Tonya was chosen as "Senior of the Month." She was asked to speak to the school board about her school. She does intend to go to college, but is thinking of enrolling in the Job Corps first, saving money, and then attending college. When asked about what she might want to do for a career, she said, "I love the stars. I might study astronomy. I also like criminal justice. I love computers. I like music and art. I plan to go into graphic art. There's so many things I want to do."

Tonya also credits her friends for helping her turn her life around. She said she had some friends that were a negative influence but others that "told me it wasn't worth doing drugs and alcohol, to think about my future, and that the only way you can have respect from others is to do things for yourself." One friend in particular, who had already graduated from the alternative school, helped Tonya. "She was much older than I am, five years older, and she helped me get on the right track. She'd say, 'I'll pick you up at school. And I'll take you to school.' She'd like be 'mom.' And I found love and respect [from her] and my other friends at school."

Tonya's advice to adults who want to help kids bounce back is partially based on her experiences in in-patient therapy programs that she didn't find helpful. She said adults should "take it one step at a time. You know, you

"I'm so proud of myself, I just want to keep going."

can't reach kids by pulling them in, you can't just throw out a rope and pull them in. You have to be steady and just take it easy. You have to wait. It's like putting a trap out for them, and you know, they'll keep coming closer and closer. And finally, you'll catch them." The bait, she added, is "love and respect." Most kids that are doing alcohol and other drugs experience a lack of respect and support, she said.

Tonya still can't quite believe the way her life turned around, including "getting As and Bs and I used to have Ds and Fs all the time. It surprises me, especially when people want to interview me and take me places. I'm like, 'Are you sure it's me?' I'm surprised at myself too. But I'm so proud of myself, I just want to keep going." ✳

Nan Henderson, M.S.W., is a national speaker and consultant on fostering resiliency and wellness, alcohol and other drug issues, and on organizational change. She has co-authored/edited five books about resiliency, and is the Editor-in-chief at Resiliency In Action, Inc. She can be reached at Nan Henderson and Associates, 5130 La Jolla Blvd., #2K, San Diego, CA 92109, p/f (858-488-5034), or by e-mail: (nanh@connectnet.com).

PART FOUR

Creating Safe/Disciplined Schools

How We Revised Our School Policy to Foster Resiliency

by Georgia Stevens, L.P.C.C.

In the narrative below, school counselor Georgia Stevens details the changes in policy initiated in Rio Rancho Elementary School in Rio Rancho, New Mexico based on staff desire to increase student resiliency. She also offers some results of her initial evaluation as to how the policy revision has changed student attitudes and behaviors.

Bonding with students while making expectations clear is a challenge we've met at our school, using a revitalized discipline program that refers students with repeated problems into social skills development.

Staff training in resiliency concepts and funding through a grant (which paid for the necessary planning time) supported the revision of our entire discipline program. Teachers wanted a program that provided more immediate incentives and consequences as well as the development of intrinsic valuing of appropriate behavior. A team of primary and intermediate teachers, along with our principal and myself, met twice for several hours one summer to create a new approach to discipline.

Responsibility was the concept we chose for focus. We wanted students to develop responsibility for themselves, their behavior, and their school. The revised rules, developed by our team, were first discussed with staff, who then discussed them with students in individual classes. They focused on disrespect toward staff and/or school property, foul language, fighting, and unsafe behavior—offenses for which discipline notices called "pink slips" are written. Pink slips can also be issued for serious harmful behavior in the classroom.

Recognition of responsible behavior is given in the revised policy to all students in classrooms where no student has received a pink slip during the previous week. The principal and myself cover playground duty at free recesses, so teachers get a break as well. Five weeks free of pink slips earn new pencils for the entire class, resulting in cheers from the students that can be heard down the school hallways! One additional incentive, carried over from our earlier policy, is also provided: A "Student of the Week" is selected by each classroom teacher, resulting in about 30 names read weekly over the intercom and awards of certificates at local fast food restaurants presented to the students. The discipline phase of the program hinges on our "Responsibility Room," where students go during a recess soon after receiving a pink slip. We have chosen to use the long recess of 30 minutes after lunch for the "Responsibility Room." Teachers volunteer to staff this room in place of playground duty, and use the time helping students understand what led up to the infraction and what would have been more appropriate behavior. Sometimes an apology is written or a plan is developed for better behavior.

The "Skill Builders" Program

Any student who receives a third pink slip is referred to Skill Builders. Occasionally, a serious infraction will result in a referral when a student has just one or two pink slips. Five consecutive lunch recesses are spent in Skill Builders, followed by four weekly "booster sessions." Middle school students and/or a role model from the referred student's classroom sometimes participate in the skills training to provide positive models and/or inter-environmental reminders of the skills. Letters to parents, signed by the teacher, counselor, and principal, describe the reasons for a student referral to the program, the skills that will be developed, and the ways parents can support the training.

The Skill Builders training is based on cognitive behavioral approaches to behavior change, engaging the students' input, using behavioral rehearsal of covert self-statements, and "body anchors."

Step One
Initially, I discuss with students what they enjoy about school and the reasons they want to avoid trouble. They generate a list of consequences they want to avoid and another list of the privileges they seek.

Step Two
Next, a list of STOP words is generated—words that students can use to tell themselves to stop long enough to think a situation through. "Relax, it's not worth a pink slip" and "settle down" are covert self-commands that students have suggested for the list. A bilingual student suggested "para" which means "stop." Another suggested "no estoy bien" which in Spanish means, "I'm not well"—a phrase that told him things are not going well and he needs to think about what to do next.

Step Three
The next step in the instruction is in consequential thinking, the THINK words. Students complete the sentence, "If I do that...." with short phrases.

Step Four
Finally the DO list is introduced, with students generating ideas about ways to handle interpersonal problems. "Walk away," "talk it out," or "tell a teacher" are typical student suggestions. Another popular idea: "get a conflict mediator"—a validation of the credibility of our school-wide mediation program.

A practice phase follows. Students usually work in pairs to generate skits demonstrating use of the skills. The student demonstrating the skill is asked to include the following "body anchors" as he or she practices:

- hold a hand up to cue the STOP step;
- put a finger on the temple to cue the THINK step;
- give a "thumbs up" sign to cue the DO step.

On Fridays students currently in the Skill Builders group meet with students from previous groups for booster sessions. During these Friday sessions, mentors from a neighboring middle school, usually seventh graders, participate by acting in the skits, joining the discussion, giving advice, and occasionally pulling individual students aside to ask how they are doing. Fridays are the time for reflection on the question: "How have you used your STOP, THINK, and DO skills?"

Students graduate from Skill Builders after they have been in school four weeks without additional pink slips. If a Skill Builder does get into trouble, he or she continues to participate in Friday booster sessions until the achievement of four trouble-free weeks. Additional pink slips result in students going through a full Skill Builders program again, followed by four booster sessions. Some students have completed the training several times, and some of these have eventually become my assistants in training other students.

The graduation from Skill Builders consists of a simple party where student participants invite a friend for ice cream or pizza and games. Though these celebrations are uncomplicated, students love them. "This is a cool party" was written on my chalkboard by one student graduate and her friend—a sentiment often expressed by other graduates.

During the school year following graduation from Skill Builders students continue to receive recognition in increasing increments for the time they stay out of trouble. Incentives are offered at four weeks, five weeks, six weeks, etc. One spring a local restaurant owner, whose son had completed the program, hosted a pizza party at the end of the school year only for students who had stayed out of trouble following their graduation from Skill Builders, as well as the seventh grade mentors. Parents and our school's DARE officer attended, and coupons for merchandize at local businesses were given out to the students at the party.

Results of the Program

Twenty-five students participated in the program during the first year it was implemented. Only 13 of those original program graduates attended our school the next year due to graduation to middle school and families moving out of the area. These 13 students received 25 percent of the pink slips issued in the first year of the program. The following year, this original group received only 12.5 percent of the pink slips issued during the year. Only five of the 13 repeated the program a second time during the second year. School-wide, the number of pink slips issued decreased by 14 percent during the second year of the program.

Further evaluation is needed to validate our anecdotal information and my personal observations that this program appears to increase students' help-seeking ability, use of a more appropriate repertoire of interpersonal skills, and the trust they have in the school staff.

Seven Essential Steps to Safer Schools

by Rick Phillips and Chris Pack

The many well-publicized school tragedies over the past four years have spawned discussions in schools and communities nationwide. Citizens everywhere naturally ask "why?" and try to figure out how to respond. It is important to recognize that violence is a complex issue with roots that stretch back many decades and touch nearly every social institution, including schools, families, law enforcement, government, the media, and business interests.

It is also important to resist the temptation to latch on to quick fixes and simple explanations — what's most visible is often just the tip of the iceberg. So while new rules and increased surveillance have a place in a comprehensive school safety plan, by themselves they cannot make schools safe. A healthy and productive garden needs more than a fence around it to keep out the deer and other unwelcome critters. It requires tilling and building the soil, attending to all the plants, and providing extra support for those that may not be flourishing. That is the way to create a resilient and thriving environment.

Ted Okey, principal at Orchard Mesa Middle School shares a table at lunch with 8th grade students. *See related chapter on page 21.*

Safe schools are built on the recognition that all youth have basic developmental needs—belonging, recognition, power, and a sense of purpose—and they embody a culture in which those needs are met in diverse and pro-social ways. Unfortunately, too many schools and communities limit their offerings to the "3As"—academics, athletics, and activities. Since many youth are not drawn to or don't excel in academics, athletics, or the more traditional activities like student government, they are left outside the mainstream, feeling disconnected and excluded. This situation warrants concern, as too many students are without connection. As a result they are at increased risk for participating in health-compromising behaviors.

Building safer schools requires engaging all youth in positive pursuits that meet their basic developmental needs. It means broadening opportunities for involvement, working more collaboratively with community agencies, encouraging youth to sit at the same table as adults, and insuring that every student hears his or her name in a positive way every day. More specifically, it requires that all youth and adults feel welcomed, respected, and understood; all have a place and know they belong. It requires a sense of shared ownership, common ground, and 'stakeholderness,' which occurs when people feel heard, have a vital role to fill, and have opportunities to participate in making decisions that impact their lives.

The challenge of maintaining a safe campus is neither easily understood nor quickly met. Rising to that challenge requires a comprehensive, community-wide effort over the long term, which countless studies prove ultimately saves time, saves money, and helps us do our job to prepare young people to be competent and compassionate contributors to our communities.

The following seven steps serve as a guide for taking prudent action to increase school safety and the overall effectiveness of educational processes.

Step 1: Build School-Community Partnerships

School violence is not a problem of schools alone. Successfully meeting the developmental needs of youth requires a comprehensive, community-wide effort best coordinated by a school-community partnership that includes law enforcement, faith groups, businesses, government, seniors, community-based and youth-serving organizations, along with students, teachers, administrators and parents.

Potential Actions: Convene the key stakeholders on a regular basis; provide them with the support they need to align behind a common vision and effectively advocate for school safety.

Step 2: Create a School Safety Team

Since students are the primary victims and perpetrators of school violence, they hold the key to whatever solutions are developed. Comprised of students, staff, teachers, administrators, school resource officers, and parents, the School Safety Team meets regularly to monitor school climate. The Team provides a forum in which all stakeholders can voice their concerns and can work with key decision-makers to implement specific actions that promote safety and prevent violence in the school.

Potential Action: Convene stakeholders to form Team; provide training and other support so the Team can function effectively.

Step 3: Provide Teacher and Staff Training

Whether they are bus drivers or classroom teachers, attendance secretaries or librarians, every adult has opportunities to notice students who are not involved, or hurting, or otherwise in need, and then to intervene. In order to utilize these opportunities, every member of the staff must have the skills to identify, reach out to, and connect with those students, and when necessary, to direct them to appropriate resources.

Potential actions: Conduct in-service training to help staff better understand their role and better utilize a full range of youth-adult relationships; focus on awareness and identification, communication skills, and referral to resources.

Step 4: Promote Tolerance and Diversity Activities

Decreasing the tension between the cliques and interest groups on a campus requires that tolerance and respect be an integral part of the school culture. By infusing the entire school with ongoing activities that promote dialogue, understanding, tolerance, and respect for differences, the school climate can be improved.

Potential Actions: Initiate guided class discussions led by specially trained students, utilize guest speakers, forums, lock-ins, trainings and other experiences; recognize youth and adults who have made positive contributions to school climate; bring in community members of different backgrounds to tell their stories.

Step 5: Offer Opportunities for the Least Engaged Youth

While all youth have the same developmental needs for belonging, recognition and power, only some youth get them met through the primary avenues of academics, athletics, and activities. Since those needs will get met, either pro-socially or otherwise, it is in the school's and students' best interest to develop other appealing and meaningful ways for meeting students' needs through school and community.

Potential Actions: Create opportunities for these students to be mentors or tutors, to learn the skills to start a business, to serve those in need, to build a skateboard park or ropes course, to plan events and other needed activities.

Step 6: Organize Youth Ambassador/Outreach Programs

Every school needs an organized team of students who are committed to and trained in awareness, communication skills, and conflict resolution skills, available on campus to be "prejudice busters," teachers of tolerance, and ambassadors of peace. These students notice, intervene, and refer where necessary.

Potential Actions: Strengthen or create peer helping programs like new-student buddy systems, conflict mediation, and teen theater.

Step 7: Increase Parent Involvement

Since parents significantly influence students' opinions, values, and interaction skills, parent understanding and support is essential for any successful school safety plan. But Booster Nights and Open Houses usually draw only the familiar faces of the highly engaged parents, so schools must find other ways to connect with parents, especially those not actively involved in their children's education.

Potential Actions: Initiate parent dialogue nights in homes to discuss safety, tolerance, and other issues, co-hosted by a parent, student, and a school-community partnership.

These steps will draw together all the actors in the school safety drama, help them align behind a common vision, and help them take effective steps to insure that schools are safe places in which young people and adults learn how to be competent and compassionate contributors to their communities. ✳

Rick Phillips and Chris Pack are the Executive Director and Program Director of Community Matters, a non-profit organization that has worked in more than 150 different communities nationwide, helping build and sustain effective partnerships, train staff and students, and engage youth in meaningful learning, leadership, and service opportunities. They can be contacted at Community Matters, P. O. Box 14816, Santa Rosa, CA 95402. Tel: (707) 823-6159. Email: team@commatters.org.

Building Resilience Through Student Assistance Programming

by Tim Duffey, M.Ed.

The Maine Department of Education Student Assistance Team Unit has trained over 320 building-based student assistance teams. The Unit has received national recognition for the strength of its programming and high quality support materials. The program has been highlighted at the National Student Assistance Conference and the National Conference for Coordinators of Homeless Children and Youth. Denver, Colorado schools recently received training in the Maine Model as a prototype of service delivery for their system. The 250-page training manual utilized to train teams is regularly mailed to all state Safe and Drug-Free Schools and Communities Coordinators. This dissemination has resulted in frequent citation of the manual's quality and comprehensive nature by student assistance professionals around the country.

The process utilized by the teams trained in the Maine model is outlined below.

1. **An Identification Process:**
   School personnel or other concerned persons initiate referral to student assistance team. Student self-referral also is possible. Referrals are based on *observable behavior.*

2. **An Intervention Process:**
   Trained student assistance team members discuss referral information and develop short term action plan outlining steps to be taken, timelines, and accountability for completion.

3. **A Referral Process:**
   Action plans indicate appropriate referrals for assistance to resources within and outside the school setting.

4. **An Implementation Process:**
   Individual team members or designated referral sources carry out recommendations. Designated team member serves as "case manager" to monitor plan implementation.

5. **A Follow-up Process:**
   Team evaluates success of intervention strategies on a regular basis. Adjustments are made as necessary.

Though the membership of Maine student assistance teams is determined by individual schools, emphasis is placed on team composition reflecting the diverse training, experience, and professional expertise available within Maine schools. Administrators, classroom teachers, nurses, school counselors, special educators, Chapter One and/or migrant educators, chemical health coordinators, and school social workers are all roles likely to be represented on local student assistance teams

(SATs). In many instances, cooperative agreements (emphasizing confidentiality) with local law enforcement and social service providers allow community professionals to add their unique backgrounds to the teams.

This multi-disciplinary approach, built upon effective team development, provides a means of operation rarely found within existing school structures. The process builds a sense of "our students" rather than "your students." This approach differs from the prevalant paradigm of student assistance, where students are identified by who is seen to have primary responsibility for them and their behavior (classroom teacher, special education, school counselor, etc.) and as a result, school staff feel isolated and overwhelmed with the nature of issues they are left to deal with... seemingly on their own.

In addition to emphasizing a multi-disciplinary approach, the Maine project's focus has evolved over time from one targeting the "at risk" population to one that emphasizes the strength and power of addressing resiliency and asset development for ALL children and youth. This change in focus reflects recent shifts in the field of prevention recognizing the potential for increased harm by labeling a child "at risk" (Benard, 1993, 1995) and the tendency to describe children "by the problems they face rather than by the strengths they possess" (Benard, 1989). The result has been a stronger alignment with resiliency and asset development research.

History of the Maine Student Assistance Project

The student assistance effort in Maine grew from a variety of sources during the 1980s. A grassroots demand by school staff to address increasing needs for alcohol and other drug services within schools led to high level dialogue by Department of Education staff. This discussion led to a statewide *Task Force Report on Affected Children* (Department of Education, 1988). Among the findings of this report was the fact that many children affected by the alcohol or other drug use, abuse, or dependency of another person in their lives were being referred to special education. Behavioral patterns of these affected children often mimicked those of learning disabled students. Such patterns often led teachers to refer these youngsters for a special education screening.

The report stated that when these students did not qualify for special education services, they often fell in the proverbial "crack" between programs. They were not succeeding in the regular education setting as currently constructed, yet they did not meet special education criteria enabling them to receive assistance from learning specialists. The Task Force recommended that a better system be developed to ensure all Maine school children receive appropriate assistance to achieve success. It was also clear that alcohol and other drug issues were not the only concern facing Maine students, families, and educators. From its earliest stages, this project was designed to be flexible enough to address the wide range of concerns facing Maine youth. To meet the needs evident within schools, this process would have to provide staff a more effective intake and referral mechanism for students *s.*

Sharon Rice, Special Education Director in Auburn, Maine, served as a member of the development and implementation team that brought the program to reality. "In addition to the physiological and neurological difficulties many children face, we must also recognize that our youth are mirrors of societal trends," she says. "They reflect the fragmentation of our culture. Our challenge is to move beyond the fragmentation into more wholeness within our entire society, of which our schools are but a single part." The program was designed to bring together key players in the educational system to meet this student need.

Department staff began to explore the potential for student assistance programs in use by other states as a means to address the varied needs of Maine students. In addition, the efforts of business and industry to improve problem solving and product delivery through the use of interdisciplinary teams was explored as a means of improved service delivery. A model began to take shape incorporating these two fields of education intervention and industrial teaming. In the process, a wide range of constituents were consulted to formulate these supportive services for Maine's children and youth. School counselors, nurses, social workers, teachers, and administrators were among those contacted for input into the model.

A hallmark of the Maine model is an emphasis on essential team skills. Skills critical for the successful formation and operation of any team-based program over an extended period of time were seen as critical tools. Meeting skills also received attention, ensuring teams access to the skills and resources needed to conduct efficient meetings. Such attention to honoring the time investment various professionals provide such an effort was a unique feature of the Maine approach to student assistance.

The resulting model was submitted to the US Department of Education (USDE) "Personnel Training Grant" process for funding consideration. In 1990, the Maine Department of Education received its first allocation of funds from the USDE to begin disseminating the model to Maine schools. The formation of the "Student Assistance Team Unit" within the Department ensured that consistency in training, technical assistance, and follow-up services were in place for schools adopting the student assistance philosophy and Maine's model for delivery.

Measures of Success

The program has utilized a variety of evaluation methods to measure the success of the project. One indicator of success is the finding that nearly 80% of trained teams continue to function beyond the first year following initial training. With the multitude of demands facing educators today, longevity of a project often reflects an investment of time and resources that provide a measure of reasonable "return on investment." In follow-up contacts, student assistance team members frequently cited a sense of accomplishment in working in these teams that they said they feel lacking in much of their work. They said they know their time will be well spent in the meetings attended and they will be among peers of a common mind working to improve conditions for all students. Also, members reported they appreciate the team focus on developing action plans that address specific, observable behaviors which enhance student performance, as well as identifying systemic issues impacting all students and staff.

The annual SAT project evaluations have uncovered other interesting results. Over half the schools surveyed indicated that referrals to special education are "more appropriate" as a result of utilizing this process. Comparison of student assistance team sites and non-SAT sites indicate that those schools having teams are more likely to have an effective referral process in place for alcohol and other drug issues. The SAT process was described as "beneficial" by 100% of those surveyed in trained sites, and "effective" by 73%. In addition, 68% of respondents indicated that a written follow-up procedure was used in the team's strategy planning (Medical Care Development, 1995). Such consistent follow-up is often lacking in student referral and intervention processes.

Resiliency Integration

Over the past few years, the Student Assistance Team Unit staff have made a concerted effort to provide local teams with a foundation in resiliency principles. This information has been viewed as essential to keep the work of this project at the forefront of effective prevention and intervention programming. Initial team training now contains a segment outlining the research on resiliency and positive youth development. References utilized focus on the work of Bonnie Benard, Peter Benson, Emmy Werner and Ruth Smith, Steve and Sybil Wolin, and Nan Henderson and Mike Milstein, among others. Regional networking meetings of existing teams have highlighted resiliency research and philosophy as well.

Unit staff are frequently called upon for resiliency-based presentations in conferences and training sessions conducted by other Department of Education staff. Their involvement has led to inclusion of resiliency principles as central tenets within several Department publications. *Fostering Hope: A Prevention Process*, developed by the Department's Prevention Team (Maine Department of Education, 1996) and the state's Improving America's Schools Act (IASA) application are two examples of documents now reflecting the resiliency paradigm. Such inclusion is reflective of Department staff members' belief that school reform and resiliency building are simultaneously achieved.

In November 1994, an historical event resulted from the resiliency foundation being built by Department of Education personnel. Nan Henderson provided a day-long resiliency training for representatives from ALL departments of state government impacting families and youth. The memo announcing the event was a piece of history in itself. This document was the first to invite staff from these departments with signatures from each of the departments' Commissioners. The workshop facilitated development of common language for all in attendance, regardless of their work unit. While bureaucracies are notoriously slow to change, the initial effort of this event is still having ripple effects. Various departments continue to converse intradepartmentally regarding the implications of resiliency research on their activities.

Sample forms provided to local teams have also undergone change to reflect the resilience-building paradigm. Student referral forms have been drastically altered from the deficit-focused forms used in the 1980s to forms balancing statements of concern (based on observable behaviors) with statements of student strengths and assets.

The sample form on the following page is one example. Developed by SAT Unit staff, it is designed to assist local SATs in building student intervention plans that align with resiliency principles. Such additions ensure that asset and resiliency development are considered in balance with behavioral concerns and are consistent with current thinking on this topic (Henderson and Milstein, 1996; Henderson, 1996). The SAT unit is currently considering a further revision of assessment forms based on two that recently appeared in the *Student Assistance Journal* (Henderson, 1996). [These are included on page 96.]

Student assistance team members are being encouraged to consider how they can effectively inform students of resiliency characteristics and assist them with identifying and describing those present in their lives. This emphasis on identification of strengths and assets versus a problem focus will impact ways of thinking for both students and staff. Protective factors identified by Hawkins and Catalano (1992), resiliency factors described by Benard (1993), [both reflected in sample action planning form], and the resiliency elements of insight, independence, relationships, initiative, humor, creativity, and morality described by the Wolins (1993) are outlined for team integration to existing efforts.

Future Trends

The Maine legislature recently approved six guiding principles recommended by the Task Force on Learning results. This structure will shape the future education for all Maine students. The student assistance process provides a critical mechanism to ensure students have the environment and structure needed to realize a readiness to learn and thereby achieve designated content standards as outlined in these principles.

The May 1996 *Report of the Governor's Task Force on Adolescent Suicide & Self-Destructive Behaviors* contained the following recommendation: *"All schools are encouraged to have student assistance teams."* This indication of support reflects the positive impact these teams have had within Maine schools. According to Roger Richards, coordinator of the Student Assistance Team Unit, "The data supporting the effectiveness of this program is resulting in an expanding role for these teams. Inclusion within the recent *Governor's Task Force Report* is a clear example." He adds, "Increasing needs of Maine students creates a growing demand for an effective response mechanism. We are seeing an ever widening professional need to work in this way for the benefit of all youth in our schools." ❊

SAMPLE
Resiliency-Based Action Planning Form

Student: _____   Grade: _____

Referred by: _____

Statement of presenting problem(s):

To enhance the quality of interventions, identify how each of the six elements of building resiliency will be addressed for this student.

Pro-Social Bonds
Identify positive connections this student currently has with people (peers & adults), programs, or activities, clubs and organizations.

Positive bonds will be fostered for this student as follows, based upon identified interests and strengths:

Social Skills
Describe strengths observed in this student's social skill development. Identify life skills training they have received/are receiving.

The social skill development of this student will be enhanced in these ways:

Clear and Consistent Boundaries
The following efforts are in place to provide clear and consistent boundaries for this student school-wide:

Clarity and consistency of boundaries school-wide will be enhanced for this student in the following ways:

Care and Support
This student is provided clear messages of care and support in the following ways:

Messages of care and support for this student will be strengthened in the following ways:

High Expectations for Success
Clear messages of high expectations for behavior and performance are provided this student in the following ways:

High expectations will be strengthened for this student by:

Meaningful Participation
This student is currently involved in the following ways that provide meaningful participation within and outside the school setting:

Meaningful participation for this student will be enhanced by:

References

Benard, B. (1993). *Turning the corner from risk to resiliency*. Portland, OR: Western Regional Center for Drug-Free Schools and Communities, Northwest Educational Laboratory.

Benard, B. (1995). How schools can foster resiliency in children. In *Western Center News*. September. Portland, OR: Western Regional Center for Drug-Free Schools and Communities, Northwest Educational Laboratory.

Hawkins, J.D., Catalano, R.F., Jr., et al. (1992). *Communities that care*. San Francisco, CA: Jossey-Bass.

Henderson, N. (1996). SAPs that build student resiliency. In *Student Assistance Journal*. March/April. Troy, MI: Performance Resource Press.

Henderson, N., & Milstein, M. (1996). *Resiliency in schools: Making it happen for students and educators*. Thousand Oaks, CA: Corwin Press.

Maine Department of Education (1988). *Task force report on affected children*. Augusta, ME.

Maine Department of Education (1994). *Student assistance team training manual*. Augusta, ME.

Maine Department of Education (1996). *Fostering hope: A prevention process*. Augusta, ME.

Medical Care Development (1995). *Maine student assistance team process evaluation, 1994*. Augusta, ME.

Office of Substance Abuse (1996). *Report of the Governor's Task Force on adolescent suicide & self-destructive behaviors*. Augusta, ME.

Wolin, S. J., & S. (1993). *The resilient self: How survivors of troubled families rise above adversity*. New York, NY: Villard Books.

Tim Duffey, M.Ed., is Past President of the National Association of Leadership for Student Assistance Programs, co-founder of the New England consulting group, Common Ground In Prevention, and a former Feature Editor of Resiliency In Action. He can be reached at Common Ground In Prevention (207-839-6319) or by e-mail: (tduffey47@aol.com).

The following forms, adapted from "SAPs that Build Student Resiliency" by Nan Henderson, which appeared in the March, 1996 Student Assistance Journal, provide additional examples of student assistance paperwork reflecting the process of integration of resiliency principles into student assistance programs.

Assessment of Environmental Resiliency-Builders

NAME OF STUDENT _____

1. Positive bond's in this student's life:
   People
   Interests/Activities
   Describe your connection to this student:
2. Situations where the student experiences structure/clear boundaries:
3. The student has learned these life skills (as evidenced by their use):
   The student is currently receiving life skills training (describe):
4. Individuals/organizations/settings that provide this student with caring and support:
5. Individuals/environmental situations that communicate high expectations for success to this student:
6. This student is involved in helping others/making positive contributions in the following ways:

How can these environmental resiliency-builders be used in intervening with this student?

Assessment of Internal Characteristics of Resiliency

NAME OF STUDENT _____

Check the following personal resiliency-builders you have observed in this student (in addition to problems). (Source: Resiliency in Schools: Making It Happen for Students and Educators by Nan Henderson and Mike Milstein, published in 1996 by Corwin Press). These are ways that individuals cope with stress and adversity in their lives, and research indicates one or more of these can be identified in every student (and in every adult).

❏ Relationships - Sociability/ability to be a friend/ability to form positive relationships
❏ Service - Gives of self in service to others and/or a cause
❏ Life Skills - Uses life skills, including good decision-making, assertiveness, and impulse control
❏ Humor - Has a good sense of humor
❏ Inner Direction - Bases choices/decisions on internal evaluation (internal locus of control)
❏ Perceptiveness - Insightful understanding of people and situations
❏ Independence - "Adaptive" distancing from unhealthy people and situations/autonomy
❏ Positive View of Personal Future - Expects a positive future
❏ Flexibility - Can adjust to change; can bend as necessary to positively cope with situations
❏ Love of Learning - Capacity for and connection to learning
❏ Self-motivation - Internal initiative and positive motivation from within
❏ Competence - Is "good at something"/personal competence
❏ Self-Worth - Feelings of self-worth and self-confidence
❏ Spirituality - Personal faith in something greater
❏ Perseverance - Keeps on despite difficulty; doesn't give up
❏ Creativity - Expresses self through artistic endeavor

(From research by Richardson, et al., 1990; Werner and Smith, 1992; Hawkins, et al., 1992; and Wolin and Wolin, 1993)

How can we further nurture/build upon these resiliency builders in this student's life?

How can they be used in intervening with this student?

Annotated

Bibliography

A Resiliency Resource Primer: Resiliency and Schools

by Bonnie Benard, M.S.W.

What follows are some of my favorites; however, this is far from an exhaustive list and many wonderful resources are not included. Also keep in mind that most of these books do not use the language of resilience but are about it nonetheless as they are focused on creating caring communities within schools that meet the developmental needs of children, youth, and adults for belonging, respect, power, and meaning.

Boyd, Julie and Dalton, Joan (1992). **I Teach: A Guide to Inspiring Classroom Leadership**. Portsmouth, NH: Heinemann. *This is a "walk your talk" book grounded in the assumption that the key to learning and human development for students is the teacher's commitment to his or her own learning and growth. Through stories, vignettes, diagrams, charts, and activities, this book honors all learning styles and builds in active participation and reflection around its key themes of empowerment, relationship-building, modeling, and creating a community of learners.*

Curwin, Richard (1992). **Rediscovering Hope: Our Greatest Teaching Strategy.** Bloomington, IN: National Educational Services. *This engaging book is premised on the belief that society's greatest risk factor is youth without hope. In compelling chapter after chapter this book offers educators the opportunity to reflect on how their school structures, policies, and practices either destroy or create hope—the key to learning and life success.*

Delpit, Lisa (1995). **Other People's Children: Cultural Conflict in the Classroom.** New York, NY: The New Press. *This book of essays pierces to the heart of how schools must change if we are to successfully educate teachers to become successful educators of children of all ethnicities and cultures. Caring relationships, high expectations, and opportunities to be heard and to participate underlie the many stories in this volume of teachers who successfully are educating across cultural differences.*

Diero, Judith (1996). **Teaching With Heart: Making Healthy Connections with Students.** Thousand Oaks, CA: Corwin Press. *This book reports the author's qualitative study of six teachers in six different high schools who are known for their positive relationships with students. Besides being rich in the voices of wonderful teachers and their students, this book identifies the nature of teacher-student relationships that make a difference, the traits, experiences, skills of these teachers; and the characteristics of schools that support nurturing.*

Fullan, Michael (1993). **Change Forces: Probing the Depths of Educational Reform.** New York, NY: Falmer Press. *This small-in-size bible of educational reform, drawing much on Peter Senge's theory of learning communities, clearly documents that educational change is inside-out change, beginning in the hearts and minds of individuals who share a vision and begin to build a critical mass that, indeed, can change the world.*

Gandara, Patricia (1995). **Over the Ivy Walls: The Educational Mobility of Low-Income Chicanos.** Albany, NY: State University of New York Press. *This qualitative study of 50 high-achieving (doctoral level) Mexican Americans from low-income families (the only one specific to this cultural group that I know of) explores how these individuals succeeded academically despite the odds and makes several recommendations for educational reforms that challenge many current assumptions—based as they are on research on middle-class European Americans students and their families. Not only is this a compelling read rich in the stories of these students, it validates the power of the school to make a difference as well as the power of a bright future—"a culture of possibility"—to motivate and sustain.*

Garbarino, James et al. (1992). **Children in Danger: Coping with the Consequences of Community Violence.** San Francisco, CA: Jossey-Bass. *After documenting, through interviews with children and caregivers and supporting research, the realities of life for children growing up in "war zones" in the U.S., the authors document the critical importance the school plays as a safe haven, with the most important factor promoting children's mental health being a caring relationship between a teacher and his or her pupils—from pre-school through high-school.*

Gibbs, Jeanne (1995). **Tribes: A New Way of Learning Together.** Sausalito, CA: CenterSource Systems. *Tribes is the best process I know for building communities in classrooms and schools that are rich in caring relationships, opportunities for participation, and high and positive expectations. This revision of her earlier manual is grounded in resiliency and incorporates new research on cooperative learning, brain compatible learning, multiple intelligences, thematic instruction, human development, and social systems. And, for all hands-on people, about half this book consists of activities.*

Henderson, Nan and Milstein, Mike (1996). **Resiliency in Schools: Making It Happen for Students and Educators.** Thousand Oaks, CA: Corwin Press. *A guide, par none, for schoolwide reform that incorporates the principles of resiliency. This book is rich with examples and tools to be used in creating resiliency-building schools. As Emmy Werner states in her Foreword, this book "should be read by all administrators, teachers, and parents concerned with the future of their children."*

Hooks, Bell (1995). **Teaching to Transgress: Education as the Practice of Freedom.** New York, NY: Routledge. *Creating learning communities wherein students are not only encouraged to challenge authority but taught to "transgress" against racial, sexual, and class boundaries in order to achieve the gift of freedom is the essence of teaching and the focus of this author's account of her life as a* *teacher and social justice activist. This book demonstrates critical pedagogy in action and how members of oppressed groups can move beyond blame to compassion and community activism.*

Institute for Education in Transformation (1992). **Voices from the Inside: A Report on Schooling from Inside the Classroom.** Claremont, CA: Claremont Graduate School. *This short report documents a study done on a school which is actually based on the voices of teachers, students, and parents (a rarity indeed!). The issue of caring relationships is raised as the Number One concern of these groups and identified by them as the root cause of lowered achievement, high dropout rates, and burned-out teachers. Ironically, the evaluation process used in studying this school, based as it was in an empowerment process, actually began a process of school and classroom transformation.*

Journal for A Just and Caring Education (began January 1995). Thousand Oaks, CA: Corwin Press. *A wonderful journal whose mission "is to develop the idea of schools as sanctuaries in a tumultuous world and to promote the right of all children to a just and caring education." It focuses "on what schools can do to ensure that all children are valued, have a safe and secure environment in which to learn, and have opportunities to experience kindness and cooperation."*

Kohl, Herb (1994). **I Won't Learn from You.** New York, NY: The New Press. *Titled after his powerful essay which documents the phenomenon of refusing to learn (i.e., resistance) when a student's intelligence, dignity, or integrity is compromised by a teacher, an institution, or a larger social mindset, this book of five essays takes on—in Kohl's passionate and compelling style—all the Big Ones: Hope, Excellence, Equality, Equity, Democracy in Education. Especially great are his discussions of how caring teachers must "creatively maladjust" (requires all the resiliency traits!) to work in dysfunctional systems—and his passionate discourse on the at-risk label.*

Kohn, Alfie (1993). **The Brighter Side of Human Nature: Altruism and Empathy in Everday Life.** New York, NY: Basic Books. *Kohn definitely makes the case—supported as always by tons of research—that schools that promote the development of caring offer the hope of personal and social transformation. All of Kohn's books support the resiliency perspective and provide research documentation extraordinaire (also see his books,* **No Contest: The Case Against Competition** *and* **Punished By Rewards: The Trouble with Gold Stars, Incentive Plans, A's, Praise, and Other Bribes***).*

McCombs, Barbara and Pope, James (1995). **Motivating Hard to Reach Students.** Hyattsville, MD: American Psychology Association. *Operating from the assumption that all students are motivated to learn under the right conditions, this interactive book helps the teacher to create these conditions (i.e., protective factors) in the classroom. It also explains a process for helping students understand how their own conditioned thoughts interfere with accessing their innate resilience, motivation, and desire to learn.*

Meier, Deborah (1995). **The Power of Their Ideas: Lessons for America from a Small School in Harlem.** Boston, MA: Beacon Press. *Meier, nationally known for "turning around" an inner-city, culturally diverse high school in Harlem (where 90% of the students now graduate and 90% of those go on to college), tells her remarkable story in this book. For any skeptics asking if resiliency-focused school reform works, give them this book. Also a critical pedagogist, Meier argues for education that is caring, built on community, based on questioning and critical thinking, grounded in high expectations for all in students, and participation by all—including parents and community.*

Moffet, James (1994). **The Universal Schoolhouse: Spiritual Awakening through Education.** San Francisco, CA: Jossey-Bass. *Moffet challenges the school reform movement to reach beyond bureaucratic and corporate interests and to take on a more transformative mission by creating education that centers on personal growth, including growth of the spirit—education that enables students to adapt and thrive in spite of societal challenges and technological change. The structure for this visionary education is decentralized community-learning networks which, in essence, serve to rebuild community between young and old.*

Munson, Patricia (1991). **Winning Teachers: Teaching Winners.** Santa Cruz, CA: ETR Associates. *I love this little book focused on teacher's self-esteem (i.e., resiliency) as the key to successful school change. Filled with vignettes, pithy statements, and lots of passion, this book is a real boost to educators' self-esteem!*

Noddings, Nel (1992). **The Challenge to Care in Schools: An Alternative Approach to Education.** New York, NY: Teachers College Press. *An absolutely essential book and the "classic" on what a caring school looks like. Noddings creates a vision of a school system built on the central mission of caring (which in her model incorporates the other protective factors of high expectations and opportunities for participation) and which is organized around centers of care: care for self, for intimate others, for associates and friends, for distant others, for nonhuman animals, for plants and the physical environment, for the human-made world of objects and instruments, and for ideas.*

Polakow, Valerie (1993). **Lives on the Edge: Single Mothers and their Children in the Other America.** Chicago, IL: University of Chicago Press. *Using the language of "at promise" (i.e., resilience), this powerful and eloquent book takes on not only the "at-risk" label but shows in classroom vignette after vignette how a teacher's high or low expectations either create possibility and hope or resignation and despair for poor children of color in inner-city schools. "An ethic of caring and a new way of seeing" the strengths of poor children and their families are the keys to successfully educating and empowering our children in these contexts and "for the unmaking of poverty and the Other America."*

Seligman, Martin et al. (1995). **The Optimistic Child: A Revolutionary Program that Safeguards Children Against Depression and Builds Lifelong Resilience.** New York: Houghton Mifflin. *This book by a premier psychologist provides a step-by-step process for parents and teachers to teach children the skills* *of that powerful resilience trait, optimism—the metacognitive skills to change conditioned thinking and the social skills that will help children be connected to others. Seligman makes the convincing case that this approach can transform helplessness into mastery and reduce the risk of depression. It can also boost school performance, improve physical health, and provide children with the sense of autonomy they need to approach their teenage years.*

Sergiovanni, Thomas (1993). **Building Community in Schools.** San Francisco, CA: Jossey-Bass. *The essential book for administrators on fostering resiliency in schools written by the premier authority on principalship. Sergiovanni challenges educators to change their basic metaphor for schooling to that of community-building, which means changing their basic thoughts and beliefs about students, teachers, and parents. "If we want to rewrite the script to enable good schools to flourish, we need to rebuild community." This book guides the way.*

Stewart, Darlene (1991). **Creating the Teachable Moment: An Innovative Approach to Teaching and Learning.** Blue Ridge Summit, PA: TAB Books. *Applying metacognitive psychology to working with students, this book helps teachers and counselors to understand the role their own thinking and moods makes in creating a positive climate for learning. Illustrated through her personal story and the stories of students she's worked with, Stewart presents an approach grounded in the principles of caring relationships, high expectations, and reciprocity—and shows how easy and fun teaching can be from this perspective.*

Swadener, Beth Blue and Lubeck, Sally, eds. (1995). **Children and Families "at Promise": Deconstructing the Discourse of Risk.** Albany, NY: State University of New York Press. *The thirteen articles in this volume provide a powerful collection of both policy analysis and descriptive research studies capturing classroom" success stories" of survival, wisdom, courage, and strength in the face of apparent overwhelming odds. This book makes an eloquent plea for reframing the discourse that surrounds children and families who are poor, of color, and/or native speakers of languages other than English.*

Wang, Margaret and Gordon, Edmund, eds. (1994). **Educational Resilience in Inner-City America: Challenges and Prospects.** Hillsdale, NJ: Lawrence Erlbaum Associates. *This edited volume is a must for anyone studying resilience in schools and for anyone in a position to shape public policy or deliver educational and human services, especially to urban schools. It offers numerous suggestions for furthering a research agenda focused on the study of resilience in schools.* ✳

About the Editors of this Book

Nan Henderson, M.S.W., Bonnie Benard, M.S.W., and Nancy Sharp-Light share a strong commitment to shifting the national emphasis on "risk" to a recognition of the reality of resiliency. In 1996, drawing upon their combined backgrounds in social work, education, journalism, and business, they cofounded Resiliency In Action, Inc. The philosophy of the company, articulated by the three founders, is "resiliency is an innate self-righting and transcending ability within all children, youth, adults, organizations, and communities." The company mission is "to foster resiliency by disseminating resiliency-related information, facilitating the practical application and evaluation of the resiliency paradigm, and sustaining a national and international grass roots resiliency network."

Nan Henderson has been a clinical and school social worker; a statewide, citywide, and districtwide prevention program director; and a faculty member at several colleges and universities. She lives in San Diego, California, and now works as a consultant and speaker on fostering resiliency and wellness, and on school and organizational change. She is the coauthor of *Resiliency In Schools: Making it Happen for Students and Educators*, published in 1996 by Corwin Press; co-editor of *Resiliency In Action: Practical Ideas for Overcoming Risks and Building Strengths in Youth, Families, and Communities*, published in 1999 by Resiliency In Action, Inc.; and frequently contributes to national publications on the topic of resiliency. In 1997 she developed *The Resiliency Training Program*™, a training of trainers that has been used to train several hundred individuals from across the U.S. and other parts of the world.

Bonnie Benard has worked in the field of youth prevention for more than 20 years. She is widely recognized as a pioneer in the practical dissemination of social science research relevant to the well-being of children and youth, and currently lives in Berkeley, California. She has authored numerous publications on the prevention of youth risk behaviors and on fostering resiliency, including *Fostering Resiliency in Kids: Protective Factors in Family, School, and Community* and *Turning the Corner from Risk to Resiliency*. She is also co-editor of *Resiliency In Action: Practical Ideas for Overcoming Risks and Building Strengths in Youth, Families, and Communities*, published in 1999 by Resiliency In Action, Inc.; a frequent contributor to national publications; and a speaker and consultant on fostering resiliency and wellness in children, youth, and families.

Nancy Sharp-Light has been in the field of education since 1972 as a teacher, prevention counselor, and director of substance abuse prevention programs. She lives in Rio Rancho, New Mexico, where she now works as an educational consultant, writer, and national trainer. She is co-editor of *Resiliency In Action: Practical Ideas for Overcoming Risks and Building Strengths in Youth, Families, and Communities*, published in 1999 by Resiliency In Action, Inc.; and has written numerous curriculum, including a community-based program for substance abusing adolescents and their families, which won several awards. Her resiliency-promoting parenting curriculum, *We're Doing the Best We Can*, is the result of her many years working with multi-cultural populations in New Mexico and across the country. In 1988, she was selected as the outstanding teacher in the state of New Mexico.

Speeches, Presentations, and Training
From The Editors at Resiliency In Action, Inc.

Nan Henderson, M.S.W.: *Nan Henderson and Associates, 5130 La Jolla Blvd., #2K, San Diego, CA 92109, t/f (858) 488-5034; nanh@connectnet.com*

- "How Families, Schools, and Communities Foster Resilient Children"
- "Resiliency in Schools and other Organizations: Making it Happen"
- "Teaching Youth and Adults About Their Resiliency"
- "*The Resiliency Training Program*™ Training of Trainers

Craig Noonan, Ph.D.: *Alternatives, 5130 La Jolla Blvd., #2K, San Diego, CA 92109, t/f (858) 488-5034; wnoonan@popmail.ucsd.edu*

- "Integrating Resiliency and Effective Counseling Practice"
- "No Fault Counseling: How People Change Problematic Behavior"
- "Empowering and Effective Brief Intervention"
- "A Step-by-Step Guide to Program Evaluation"

Nancy Sharp-Light: *Sharp-Light Consulting, 602 San Juan de Rio, Rio Rancho, NM 87124 t/f(505) 891-1350; nslight@aol.com (or nslight@RTgraphics.com)*

- "Team-Building for Resilience"
- "Classroom Techniques for Moving Students from Stress to Success "
- "KidBitz: How to Present Anything to Anyone." For youth involved in any activities, such as Service-Learning Projects, requiring public contacts and presentations.

PRODUCT INFORMATION

RESILIENCY IN ACTION: *Practical Ideas for Over-coming Risks and Building Strengths in Youth, Families, & Communities*

Nan Henderson, Bonnie Benard, Nancy Sharp-Light, ed.
Foreword by Peter Benson, Ph.D., President of Search Institute
1999, 180 pages, 2nd Printing (Paperback)

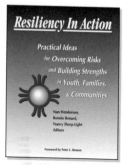

- *"Bursting with new ideas, exemplars of best practices...and interviews with individuals–leaders and pioneers in the field–who have been doing resiliency work for years. Ahead of the curve."*
  —**Dennis Saleeby, Ph.D.**, University of Kansas, Editor of *The Strengths Perspective in Social Work Practice*
- *"This is the bible for our work!"*
  —**Barbara Keller**, Executive Director, Suffolk Coalition to Prevent Alcohol and Drug Dependencies, Happauge, NY
- *"A resource that changes hearts and minds."*
  —**Brenda Holben**, Safe and Drug-Free Schools Coordinator, Cherry Creek Schools, CO

Single Copy
$28.95
ISBN 0-9669394-0-9

A one-of-a-kind resource to guide every aspect of fostering resiliency in children, youth, families, and communities. Contents include: The Foundations of Resiliency; Resiliency and Schools; Resiliency and Communities; Creating Connections: Mentoring, Support, and Peer Programs; Resiliency and Youth (including asset) Development; and Resiliency and Families. Each section is filled with easy-to-understand research reports and ways that the research is being applied. The "must have" book for schools, agencies, and community organizations as they meet the challenges of the next decade.

SCHOOLWIDE APPROACHES FOR FOSTERING RESILIENCY

Nan Henderson, Bonnie Benard, Nancy Sharp-Light, ed.
Introduction by Barbara Wotherspoon, School Principal, Newton, NH
1999, 109 pages (Paperback)

How do schools currently build resiliency in students and staff, and how can they do the job better? Based on the research-proven assumption that "effective education" and "fostering resiliency" go hand-in-hand, this book offers

- practical steps all schools can take to foster resiliency in students and staff
- an understanding of how building resiliency is the foundation of effective education, and vice versa
- resiliency-building perspectives from principals
- teaching strategies that are proven resiliency builders
- ways to assess and improve schoolwide resiliency building
- suggestions for creating safe, violence-free schools
- an annotated bibliography

Single Copy
$12.95
ISBN 0-9669394-2-5

Originally published as articles in the journal *Resiliency In Action*, this book also contains new, never-before published information.

PRODUCT INFORMATION

Mentoring for Resiliency: *Setting Up Programs to Move Youth from "Stressed to Success"*

Nan Henderson, Bonnie Benard, Nancy Sharp-Light, ed.
Introduction by Emmy Werner, Ph.D., University of California
1999, 90 pages, (Paperback)

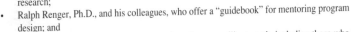

What are the crucial elements of all successful mentoring programs? This book has the answers from

- Marc Freedman, M.A., considered the "guru" of the mentoring movement;
- Bonnie Benard, M.S.W., the most widely read author on resiliency in the U.S.;
- Emmy Werner, Ph.D., known as the "mother" of resiliency research;
- Ralph Renger, Ph.D., and his colleagues, who offer a "guidebook" for mentoring program design; and
- Nan Henderson, M.S.W., who has interviewed many resilient youth–including those who have bounced back from risk behavior due to the relationships they had with mentors.
    Originally published as articles in the journal *Resiliency In Action*, this book also contains new, never-before published information.

Single Copy
$12.95

ISBN 0-9669394-1-7

Four Steps to Resiliency... the pamphlet you've been waiting for!

$25.00 per package of 50

Nan Henderson, M.S.W
Pamphlets in packages of 50

This is the pamphlet our readers have been asking for! In down-to-earth language, resiliency is defined, and four important steps anyone can take to foster resiliency in others are presented. Illustrated. Includes bibliography for further reading. Order for parents, educators, law makers, community groups, and youth.

Back issues of the journal *Resiliency In Action*

This quarterly journal is now discontinued but all back issues are available—some may be photocopied.
$7.00 each (original and photocopied)

- Premier Issue: Foundations of Resiliency
- Resiliency and Schools
- Resiliency and Communities
- Creating Connections for Resiliency: Mentoring, Support, and Peer Programs
- Resiliency and Youth Development
- Resiliency and Families
- Resiliency and the Mind-Body Connection
- Resiliency and Gender

- Changing the "At Risk" Paradigm
- Resiliency and the Arts
- Resiliency and Gender
- Resiliency and Politics
- Werner Research Update/Service Learning
- "It Takes a Child to Raise a Whole Village"/ Resiliency in Prisons
- Resiliency and Self-Esteem/Adolescence from a Strength Perspective

---

TO ORDER SEE PAGE 109

ORDER FORM

MAIL *WITH YOUR* **PO** *TO:*
    RESILIENCY IN ACTION
    P.O. BOX 90319
    SAN DIEGO, CA 92169-2819
OR **FAX** *WITH YOUR* **PO** *TO:*
    (858) 581-9231
OR **CALL TOLL FREE:**
    (800) 440-5171
OR ORDER **ON-LINE** *AT:*
    WWW.RESILIENCY.COM

Quantity Discounts		
1-10	Copies:	Price as listed
11-25	Copies of the same title:	10% discount
26-50	Copies of the same title:	20% discount
51+	Copies of the same title	25% discount

FED. ID #85-0438768

PLEASE PRINT!

Qty.	Unit Price	Description	Price

PLEASE REMEMBER TO ADD 15%

SHIPPING AND HANDLING

TO EACH ORDER

TOTAL ORDER	
15% S/H	
SUBTOTAL	
CA RESIDENTS ADD TAX 7.25%	
TOTAL AMOUNT DUE	

PLEASE SHIP TO :   *PLEASE PRINT!*

NAME _____

ORGANIZATION _____

ADDRESS _____

CITY _____ STATE _____ ZIP _____

PHONE ( ) _____ FAX ( ) _____

E-MAIL _____ PROFESSION _____

BILL TO (IF DIFFERENT) : (PLEASE ATTACH PO TO THIS FORM)

ORGANIZATION _____

ATTN. _____

ADDRESS _____

CITY _____ STATE _____ ZIP _____

PHONE ( ) _____ FAX ( ) _____

E-MAIL _____

METHOD OF PAYMENT :

☐ CHECK ENCLOSED (CK # _____)

☐ PURCHASE ORDER ATTACHED: PO# _____

☐ CREDIT CARD

MC ☐ MasterCard V ☐ VISA

CC# _____ EXP. DATE _____

CARD HOLDER'S SIGNATURE _____